1991

Everything You Needed to Learn about Writing in High School — But

EVERYTHING YOU NEEDED TO LEARN ABOUT WRITING IN HIGH SCHOOL– BUT

a) you were in love

b) you have forgotten

c) you fell asleep

d) they didn't tell you

e) all of the above

BETH MEANS
and
LINDY LINDNER

Illustrated by
Don Gronning

1989
LIBRARIES UNLIMITED, INC.
Englewood, Colorado

LIBRARIES UNLIMITED, INC.
P.O. Box 3988
Englewood, Colorado 80155-3988

Library of Congress Cataloging-in-Publication Data

Means, Beth, 1949-
   Everything you needed to learn about writing in high school--but
(a) you were in love; (b) you have forgotten; (c) you fell asleep;
(d) they didn't tell you; (e) all of the above /
Beth Means and Lindy Lindner ; illustrated by Don Gronning.
   xv, 180 p. 17x25 cm.
   Includes bibliographical references.
   ISBN 0-87287-711-6
   1. English language--Rhetoric.   I. Lindner, Lindy, 1945-
II. Title.
PE1408.M435   1989
808'.042--dc20   89-13156
                                                           CIP

For Martha
best friends always

With special thanks to Marcia Olsen, Anne Helmholz, and Martha Means; and Dr. Anita Francis for patient reading and testing; to Caroline Lacy Turner, our long-suffering bird dog on sources and errors; to David Loertscher and Carmel Huestis for editorial advice beyond the call of duty; to Henriette Klauser for freeing the artist within and Betty Hagman for training the craftsman, and finally to all the writers from Virgil to Gary Paulsen who wittingly or unwittingly came along for the ride.

Contents

5 – EDITING WITH ENTHUSIASM *(continued)*

Foreword

Do you like living on the edge? A way with words is the way to do it. Words shape our world. What are treaties but words: written words binding nations. What is the Constitution but words: words of inspiration and direction. What is the ad for toothpaste that makes you buy, the brief in court that sends a criminal to prison, the resume that gets the job, the proposal that secures the promotion, the love letter that wins your sweetheart's affection but words; words to woo, to persuade, to entertain, to teach. A way with words is a way with life, a way to live life to its fullest, to know yourself deeply, to share yourself significantly, and a way to make a difference in our world.

Words are an interior gift as well as a gift we give to others. Power over words is power over yourself, a way to access the central core. The beauty of writing is that it taps into that part of your brain that does not know, what philosophers call "knowing without knowing": sitting down before a blank piece of paper and knowing what you want to say but not knowing how to say it. Perhaps you were trained not to begin until you knew what you were going to say; some say you cannot even start a piece until you know how it will end. I say let the writing explore the options with you. Instead of staring at a blank page, let the writing release your unknowing, the very act of writing it down frees the expression lodged in your mind. Do not wait to write until you know it all. Waiting to write until you know it all is paralyzing, because sometimes we don't know the ending before we begin, and sometimes—curious but just as true— sometimes we don't know the beginning until we come to the end. Words on paper are not meant to be a record of crystallized thought; they are the search for thought in motion, and the best writing takes the reader along on the adventure with a sense of wonder and exploration.

Writing is a process. As I would put it, it takes two halves of the brain. To make writing both fluent and fun, separate those two, using each in its respective strength at the appropriate time. Write first, then edit; that is the key to writing well and to enjoying what you write. Yet it is difficult to strike a balance. Too much emphasis on structure and form can discourage and stultify, too much freedom of expression can influence the final impact. We need heart and head—passion, yes, but passion tempered with form. How to draw the line? And where to?

These are questions that I continue to grapple with in my own work: how to harness enthusiasm and flame the pilot light of inspiration, and yet pay attention to structure and form—how to discipline and not dishearten, how to fill writers' hearts with confidence, cheerlead them on and yet challenge them to the pruning part, the part that takes the inspired ideas and respects the reader enough to present those ideas in a way that transfers the passion and the thought to an audience. And finally how to arrive at a stage where the two parts of the process meld into one, where craft and art are a seamless garment, a stage where the electrical impulses between right and left brain travel so fast and furiously as to crackle in midair with the excitement of discovery.

This gentle, encouraging, supportive book provides such a bridge. Beth Means and Lindy Lindner, real-life writer, daily life teacher, are the perfect pair to present a book about learning to write. First, they energize and inspire you and turn you into—Superwriter! Look up in the sky! Able to dash off term papers, job resumes, love letters, and memos with a single nonstop stroke of the pen! Able to lift high spirits with words of inspiration and fervor. Able to leap over the mundane and trivial with a single bound.

Write, write, write, and keep on writing—and when you have written, do not be afraid to edit. Beth and Lindy show you how to hone your words, to carve and shape your sentences so your finished piece will have the kind of effect you want. You will be amazed at your own talent—your speed, your fluency, your impact. They will goad you and guide you. Like a good coach, these two authors challenge you to hard work, while instilling belief that you are equal to that challenge.

Who knows what power such a process will unleash? Who knows what untapped worlds you will discover and lead others to with your writing? These two gentle guides have come to support you and encourage you and give you instructions. Me? I am standing by the sidelines cheering you on. Actually, more appropriate, I am running alongside you, learning with you about my expanded world as together we explore the power of the pen. The world is waiting for your words—to amuse, to entertain, to persuade, to move to tears, to tickle with laughter and glee, to giggle, to cry. This book will set you on fire. It could put some danger in your life.

HENRIETTE ANNE KLAUSER, Ph.D.
Author of *Writing on Both Sides of the Brain*

Introduction

To those who dozed their way through Nathaniel Hawthorne and punctuation lessons in high school — and didn't we all — the emphasis on writing in college and on the job comes as a shock. People soon grow anxious about writing. "I wish I had paid more attention," they chide themselves. "I should do something about my writing, but what? Study grammar? Take a creative writing course? Hire a tutor? Buy a book on writing? Which one? If you have held this conversation with yourself, you just bought the right book. Although we don't cover such details as using the subjunctive or using commas in quotations, we do try to fill in a few gaps in your background and to provide you with practical tips to make writing easier and help you achieve better results. The book pays special attention to the needs of college students but anyone writing for school, work, or pleasure should find nuggets to help them. We also point out additional resources so that you know where to look to find more detailed information on research, techniques, style questions, punctuation, or other areas you may wish to pursue in more depth.

To be honest, your high school and college English teachers probably did not mention many of the things we cover because we gathered our suggestions not from teachers, but from writers. We felt that those who write every day would give the most down-to-earth advice.

In the end, people learn to write well by writing. There is no other way. The more you write, the greater the variety of your projects; and the more enthusiasm you give each piece, the better your writing will be. Writing shouldn't be all hard work. The best writing is a joyous exploration of life. Few pleasures are so sweet as honest self-expression on paper. You can see your thoughts for the very first time. You own them. You can admire them or rearrange them to suit a whim. Discovering the joy in writing is vital to your progress. Seek it always. You will write more and grow faster.

We've arranged this book into five long chapters roughly defining the steps of a writing process:

1. Deciding what to write about

2. Planning

3. Getting words on paper

4. Drafting and editing — a few techniques

5. Editing (revision and polishing)

Breaking your writing projects into the stages of a writing process and taking it one step at a time makes writing much easier, and improves the quality of your writing as well. If you haven't used a writing process before, start now. With practice, you can adjust the steps to suit your own style. Although this is not a book on writing term papers, learning to use the writing process should help you write term papers because it helps with every kind of writing you do.

Because students are busy and want to get to work quickly, we've organized each chapter as a series of activities that we call springboards. Each springboard has specific ideas, lists, or exercises to help you with a small part of the writing process. We tried to collect fairly simple activities which seem to help most beginning writers, beginning in the sense of people who take writing seriously but who have not written or perhaps published extensively. You won't need to do every springboard. Skim through the book and choose those which most inspire you. You can use most of them over and over. Sprinkled here and there are "Student's Notebook" sections with tips on studying and writing and "Notes from the Pros" sections with suggestions from professional writers.

Before you turn to Chapter 1, we have a few pieces of general advice. First of all, whether you apply the ideas in this to school assignments or your own writing is up to you. But don't limit yourself. You may learn about history or engineering through school papers, but it may take a science fiction story or a how-to article on your favorite hobby to teach you the thrill of writing. You are, after all, a person, not a pop bottle waiting on the assembly line to be filled with education, labelled, and spit out the door in four years. Of all the things you learn in school, writing may be the most uniquely personal. Tailor it; manage your learning to suit you.

Second, do a thorough cleaning of your mental closet. Throw out all those old half-remembered style rules and vague anxieties about grammar. We mean it. Junk them completely. They only bring trouble. For example, you may have heard the style rule "use a variety of words" at some point but remember it as "never repeat a word." The first rule is good; the second disastrous. Good writers repeat words all the time for emphasis, rhythm, clarity, and to make graceful transitions. You may also feel vaguely nervous about the word *you* as you write. Wasn't there something about avoiding *you*? The full rule is to avoid *you* unless speaking directly to a reader. Avoiding it altogether could turn a perfectly clear set of instructions into scrambled eggs. Some types of writing demand the second person. Cluttering your writing with such misunderstandings could destroy your work. Start clean. Begin with one simple goal: to write what *you* would enjoy reading. Do you enjoy authors who ramble on without saying much, who throw around jargon to show off, who scramble sentences, and who wander from point to point in an organizational tangle? No, of course not. You'll only fall into such traps if you fail to write what you would read. No rule about writing can replace your own common sense. Keep your rules simple: write what you would enjoy reading; always give it your best; and get help when you need it. These rules cover almost every writing question.

You may feel frustrated with writing at times, but don't become discouraged. You will never know all that you would like to know. Only amateurs think they know it all; experts have no such illusions. Whatever its practical uses, writing is still both an art and a craft. The art comes from the creative inspiration of the writer, the craft from a long apprenticeship. This applies to every kind of writing, from the engineering report to the novel, because all writing is creative. Just keep working at it and one day you will find that you have given yourself a gift, a gift that will help you to propose ideas, motivate others, express your opinions, organize your thoughts, analyze problems, and explore the world around you. Few gifts in life are so precious.

Chapter 1

Deciding What to Write About

Waiting for inspiration is like waiting for friends. If you sit around the house and don't go out and meet them, they will never come. You have to make things happen. Writing is an active occupation, not a passive one.

— Judy Delton

INTRODUCTION

Telling a writer staring at a blank sheet of paper to "avoid the passive tense" or "use topic sentences" is like telling a knight facing a fire-breathing dragon to polish his armor. If you want to learn to write well, first relax. Forget about grammar, spelling, punctuation, style rules, and other worries for awhile. Until you can fill that blank page with words, knowing where to put the commas won't matter much. Learn to tame the dragon first; then learn to do it with style.

The good news is that you don't need to be a literary genius to slay blank pages with a flick of your pen. You just need to arm yourself with a few necessary weapons and learn a few basic battle tactics, and you can write with pleasure and verve. That's what the first three chapters of this book are about — Dragonslaying 101, 102, and 103.

Finding a Writing Idea

This chapter deals with the number one complaint of most beginning writers: they cannot think of anything to write about. Even when a professor assigns a subject or a topic, students puzzle over what to say and how to approach it. After all, writing is not just a matter of throwing any old words on the page. You want to say something. You want to put your *ideas*, not just words, on paper.

To fill the blank page, you must first find some ideas to express. There is a trick to this: instead of writing down every conceivable thought rattling through your head, first try to come up with just one good idea. We call this one central idea your "writing idea." It describes what you are going to write about in a few words. It helps you picture the whole story, article, or essay. The picture may be fuzzy at first, but it's a beginning. Once you have one clear idea, you will find that everything else — the organization, the words, the style — will come more easily.

It is a bit difficult to define exactly what makes a good writing idea, so it helps to think of a writing idea as a triangle.

The Writing Idea Triangle

The subject determines the background to the piece. It sets some broad boundaries on the information or themes to be covered. The type of plan provides a sense of direction or organization of the piece. Finally, the other elements of the writing sharpen the focus.

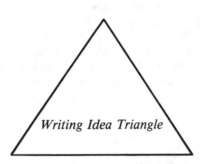

Subject

Writing Idea Triangle

Type or Plan
(e.g., fiction, nonfiction,
a genre, an outline, etc.)

Other elements of
writing (e.g., mood, the
purpose, setting, charac-
ters, audience, etc.)

When you create writing ideas, any point of the triangle can serve as a starting point, but two points and usually all three are needed to make a workable writing idea. For example, one subject can spark an infinite number of writing ideas. The subject may be horses, but the writing idea needs something more:

a character: a story about a horse named Looney Tune

a setting: a story about a horse ranch

an explanation: how to groom a horse

an opinion: why I don't like horses

a question: what was the economic importance of horses to the 19th century?

a design: descriptions of horse breeds arranged alphabetically by name

The writing idea may come from the type of writing. When we asked a group of students who were studying ancient Egypt for writing ideas about the pyramids, they came up with:

a story: a day in the life of an Egyptian pyramid-builder

a how-to: how to build a pyramid

an explanation: why the Egyptians built pyramids

tips: five problems with building a pyramid in your backyard

The other elements of the writing, such as the mood, the audience, or the characters, focus the writing idea even more tightly. For example, "A day in the life of an Egyptian pyramid-builder" can be an off-the-wall spoof or a serious historical treatise depending on the writer's choice of audience and mood.

A teacher or a publisher may assign the starting point, but finding the writing idea is *always* the responsibility of the writer. If you are writing about assigned topics, keep in mind that even a very closely defined topic is just a starting point for finding writing ideas—a small subject. Why did Hannibal fail as a military leader?

Hannibal failed because he ran out of money.

Hannibal failed because he was too far from home.

Hannibal failed because his men didn't like him.

What about Will Cuppy's wonderful idea:

Hannibal failed because he refused to admit that elephants always run backward in the face of enemy fire.

Some people insist that you should have a writing idea—even an outline—before you begin. Not true. Sometimes, it works just as well to begin writing without any preconceptions. But when you start without a writing idea, you are going after the blank page dragon bare-handed. Even David took a rock along to meet Goliath. A writing idea is a handy tool. It's your rock.

FINDING YOUR OWN STARTING POINTS

If you tell yourself, "I want a writing idea right now," your imagination may take a sudden vacation and go blank. The mind is a funny beast. It doesn't respond well to commands. Lighten up! You are not writing *War and Peace*. You are just trying to write something. You are not trying to find the perfect idea or even a complete idea. You just need a place to start. You can add to it, shape it, or change it as you go along. As one song writer put it, writing a love song is hard, but writing a love song about a woman in a red dress who has just walked into a bar for the first time in many years is easy.

To create a writing idea, first choose a starting point. Any corner of the writing idea triangle—the subject, the type, or some element of the writing—will do. Make an arbitrary choice. Then choose another point of the triangle and make another arbitrary choice. Put the two choices together. Do they suggest an idea? Write it down. Subject: ballet shoes. Type: how-to. Writing idea: how to buy ballet shoes.

Once you get the knack of finding writing ideas, you'll never run out. Even if your goal is only to improve your term papers and work reports, practice at creating all sorts of writing ideas will help you learn to effectively narrow the subject and add a little pizzazz to your work. This chapter is designed to help you develop that knack. It is divided into two main sections. The springboards in the first main section help you find starting points in the world around you. Springboards in the second section help you convert any one starting point into hundreds of writing ideas.

Because students are busy, these springboards (indeed, all the ideas in this book) take just a few minutes each and help you with any kind of writing, including writing on your own or writing an assignment.

Springboard 1: Stop, Look, and Listen

There is only one trait that marks the writer. He is always watching. It's a kind of trick of mind he is born with.

— Morley Callaghan

The beauty of "Stop, Look, and Listen" is its simplicity. Anyone can do it in a minute or two. Each time you do it, you create a great list of starting points.

Before you begin, find a little notebook that fits into your pocket or purse. Whip it out to make a stop, look, and listen list any time inspiration strikes. Keep it under your pillow at night. Never leave home without it. Good ideas appear at the oddest moments but may vanish just as quickly if you wait to make a note. This irreplaceable treasury of fleeting moments will soon become your best writing resource.

Try It

Stop, get out a piece of paper or your writing ideas notebook, and write down ten things you see and ten things you hear. Don't be picky. Anything will do. Work quickly. It shouldn't take you more than a minute.

Sometimes a list of starting points will immediately suggest writing ideas. Once you finish the list, pick a few items. See if they suggest any writing ideas or questions that might become writing ideas. Note the writing ideas below your list.

EXAMPLE (made while sitting in a classroom after school one day)

Stop, Look, and Listen List

SEE	HEAR
1. desk	1. lawn mower
2. tennis shoes	2. freeway noise
3. picture of an Amazonian frog	3. pages ruffling
4. grass	4. siren

5. pencil	5. computer printer
6. sink	6. "Who put the coffee grounds in the sink?"
7. computer	7. "This place is a mess."
8. glasses	8. giggling girls
9. hand	9. whack, whack of a book cart

Writing Ideas

Desk. Why do they make those little half desks instead of full ones? Is it to cram more students in a class like passengers on a no-frill airline? Who thought up the design? This might make an interesting research piece or a good funny piece speculating on all the crazy reasons.

Siren. Survey people's attitudes towards accidents and compare their attitudes to the statistics. Are the things people fear most also statistically the most likely to happen? What are the differences?

Glasses. Visit a local optometrist to find out how glasses are made, how optometrists are trained, or why people decide to become optometrists. Write a humorous essay about coping with life when your glasses are broken. Write a paper on the history of glasses including the latest innovations in optometry.

Additional Notes

There are many ways to create stop, look, and listen lists. Try some of these variations on the theme for fun.

1. Make the lists in specific places, such as a museum, an airport, a train, a plane, or in a favorite place.

2. Make the lists at specific times, such as during a film or television show, a classroom lecture or laboratory period, during a concert, on the bus, just before bedtime or early in the morning, once during vacation, or every day at 4:35 pm.

3. Make the lists in response to any interesting piece of art, music, dance, or photography.

4. Add "ten things you think" to "ten things you see and hear."

5. If you want to go all out, by all means take pictures or make tape recordings of the items on the lists. The pictures and tapes can be used to inspire writing or to illustrate final products.

6. Try limiting the list to specific types of starting points: only things of a certain size or color; only items expressing certain principles of physics, chemistry, or math; only soft sounds, rhythmic sounds, or sounds expressing a particular mood.

Springboard 2: This Is Your Life

Writing comes more easily if you have something to say.
—Sholem Asch

There is an old rule among writers: "When you are learning to write, first write about yourself, the things you know, and your own experiences." It's still a good rule. People assume their own lives are too dull to write about, but ask published writers where their ideas came from and, time and again, they will point to some small incident in everyday life that they simply enlarged or to something they read in the newspaper or a book. Marcel Proust got the ideas for the Swann stories while dipping a cookie into a cup of tea. Agatha Christie claimed that her best ideas came while doing dishes. They discovered writing when they discovered that they didn't need to lead a special life to write.

We all need to be reminded that those stories, research papers, and books we see in the library are the creations of ordinary people like ourselves. Even the simplest life is rich with starting points for writing. The details that make fiction sing and nonfiction concrete come from the commonplace world that surrounds each of us. Because no two people lead the same life or see life the same way, each person's writing is indeed special: The writing club is open to everyone.

The questions on the worksheet below will help you settle down and examine the possibilities in your own life. It can be used over and over to explore the details that will make your writing sing.

Try It

Answer all the questions on the filesheet (p. 8). (Any time a springboard includes a list, a worksheet, or something else that you may want to store with your practice journal because it can be used over and over, we've organized it into a filesheet for easy recopying.) After you answer the question, write a paragraph or two about three or four of your answers. If you can't remember some of the past events in your life, close your eyes and put yourself on the scene. What was the temperature? What did it smell like? How old were you? What was your main interest? Spot some small visual detail you recall. If you still can't remember anything, make up an answer.

When you are finished, go over your answers and find at least three starting points. Note any writing ideas as well. Select any answer and write about it for a few minutes.

THIS IS YOUR LIFE (FILESHEET)

1. Write down anything in your life you would like to write about.

2. Name your favorite food.

3. Name the food you hate the most.

4. Name three things you like to do. Why do you like doing them?

5. Name three things you hate doing. Why do you hate doing them?

6. Name two places you especially like to be. Why do you like being there?

7. Name two places you dislike being. Why do you dislike being there?

8. If you could do anything you wanted, what would you do?

9. Name two things you have never done but would like to try.

10. What is the best thing you've ever done?

11. What is the worst thing you've ever done?

12. What is the funniest thing you've ever done?

13. Do you own a pet? If so, list some of the things your pet does. How is your pet like you?

14. Name the members of your family (or, if you prefer, your roommates). List some of the best, worst, or funniest things they have ever done.

15. Name two things that scare you.

16. Name two things that make you happy.

17. If you were in charge of the world, name three changes you would make.

18. What is your first memory.

19. List any five things you know.

20. List any five things you don't know.

21. What is your favorite book? What is the best part?

22. Now go back and answer the first question again.

23. Make up a question about your life and answer it.

Springboard 3: Borrowing Starting Points

The two most engaging powers of an author are to make new things familiar, familar things new.

—William Makepeace Thackeray

When the world around you does not serve up enough ideas, larger worlds are easily tapped at the library. This little activity is so fast and easy, yet provides such a vast pool of ideas, you'll wonder how you ever did without it.

Try It

Let any book fall open to a page and write down five words, facts, or opinions that appear on that page. You can also let it fall open to five different pages.

If you are writing on an assigned subject, use your textbook, a book on the reading list, or a collection of articles on the subject. For fun, use trash novels, your favorite books, or books you hate. Some books are especially useful. Try using at least one of the books below:

- *Dictionaries*: Any word in a dictionary can become a starting point. Special dictionaries are also intriguing. One good example is *Morris Dictionary of Word and Phrase Origins: Vol. 1, 2, 3* by William Morris and Mary Morris. It is full of fascinating information; for example, the word "motel" was invented by an architect in San Luis Obispo, California in 1925. Although "kid" means a young goat, it has been used as an affectionate name for children since Shakespeare's time. According to H. L. Mencken's *The American Language*, another useful reference, "kid" is used in American English for "co-pilot." Try subject dictionaries. Dictionaries on science, art, music, law, computers, writing, and publishing can be found in most libraries. *The People's Chronology: A Year-by-Year Record of Human Events from Prehistory to the Present*, edited by James Trager, is wonderful for historical starting points. Try *What's What*, a dictionary of pictures with the correct names for things like venetian blinds.

- *Encyclopedias*: Try short encyclopedias, such as *The New American Desk Encyclopedia* (1984) from Signet's New American Library, or use books of lists instead, such as Irving Wallace's *The Book of Lists*, Isaac Asimov's *Book of Facts*, and the International Reading Association's *The Teacher's Book of Lists*.

- *Quotations*: Books of quotations provide good starting points for writing. Most people think of *Bartlett's Familiar Quotations*, but quotation books arranged by subject are often more interesting. Good examples are the *Dictionary of Quotations* by Bergen Evans, the *International Thesaurus of Quotations* by Rhoda Thomas Tripp, and *Peter's Quotations: Ideas for Our Time* by Laurence J. Peter. There are also many books of quotations on particular subjects.

Notes from the Pros:
On the Principle of Creativity

In *The Performing Flea*, P. G. Wodehouse notes that the best story ideas almost always sound ridiculous and illustrates his point with a delightfully absurd "writing idea" version of *Hamlet*, beginning "See, there was this guy..."

When you first begin to record ideas, be sure to write the starting points or ideas down before you make *any* decisions about them. Keep in mind that you may or may not know how you want to treat the idea yet. Almost any idea can be handled as fiction or nonfiction, as a lighthearted farce or a serious research paper. At the early stages, just try to record the ideas; choose the treatment later.

Above all, remember that creativity is not killed by judging if something is brilliant or mundane, serious or silly, good or bad: all creations are subject to judgments eventually. Creativity is killed by judging too soon.

Student's Notebook:
On Practice

Beginning writers are often too hard on themselves. "I *should* be able to write well," they tell themselves. "Why is it so difficult, so uncomfortable?" They seem to forget that people are not born knowing how to write, any more than they are born knowing how to play golf or the piano. They learn to write. And they learn to write well by writing, writing, and writing some more. Learning a little theory helps, but it cannot substitute for doing it, any more than learning the rules of golf will instantly turn you into an Arnold Palmer. Feeling comfortable and competent comes only through practice.

There are two kinds of practice: practice on a small scale in an environment where mistakes don't count and practice doing complete works without mistakes. The pianist practices scales and parts of pieces, then prepares a complete piece for a performance. The golfer develops a swing on the driving range, then plays out on the course. The writer practices writing scenes, paragraphs, sentences, or techniques in a practice journal, then tackles complete stories, papers, or essays.

Buy a cheap spiral notebook to use as a practice journal. It's your driving range, a place for you to try every kind of writing from fiction to the driest academic essay. If you have trouble writing opening sentences, transitions, or descriptions, this is the place to try them first, away from critical eyes of the outside world. Your practice journal is a place where you can experiment without worrying about flops and flubs; it's also the only place where you don't need to finish a thing. After all, it's just practice.

If you practice a little every day, writing will suddenly seem easier. A three-page paper won't seem such a big project. As your confidence grows, your writing will improve. You may even find people commenting on your talent. But you will know better. Practice makes talent into something.

When you practice, don't limit your horizons. Try everything, science fiction to advertising copy. Each type of writing teaches you something new that can be applied to other types of writing.

The next time you feel frustrated with your writing, remember the three keys to practice: regular practice on a small scale; practicing to perfect complete works; and practicing a variety of types of writing. Keep at it and one day you will look back and feel startled by your improvement.

CONVERTING STARTING POINTS INTO WRITING IDEAS

The trick to finding good writing ideas is to look for many ideas and then choose the best. The remaining springboards in this chapter help you quickly develop many writing ideas from any one starting point. Don't be too serious. Play the springboards like games. The object is to come up with several writing ideas, no matter how dull or silly they sound at first. One can usually find a very good idea on any list of four or five.

Springboard 4: The Three-Minute Fastwrite

Just as appetite comes by eating, so work brings inspiration, if inspiration is not discernible at the beginning.
— Igor Stravinsky

Three minutes of concentrated writing is an amazing amount of time to a writer. Room can be found in the busiest week for three minutes every few days. A person's first thoughts on a starting point are often the most original and powerful ones. Writing itself brings the inspiration for writing.

Try It

Get out your practice journal or a piece of paper and a comfortable pen. When you fastwrite, always use pens that feel comfortable in your hand and flow freely. The quality of the tools you use affects your writing. Great big pieces of paper produce sweeping ideas; little bitty pieces of paper, tight little ideas. Flowing pens produce a sense of ease and flow; sticky ballpoints produce a sense of stop and start. Experiment with your tools to find those that feel most comfortable to you.

To do this exercise, choose any starting point and write about it as fast as you can for three minutes. Don't try to write well. (It actually helps some people to try to write *badly*.) Just write the first things that come to mind. Don't cross out. If you change your mind, add the change in the margin or at the bottom of the page.

Read through your fastwrites and note any writing ideas you have at the bottom of the page.

Additional Notes

The three-minute fastwrite has plenty of uses for both writing and study. It can be used as:

- a daily fluency exercise

- a way to get started on a new assignment

- a way to consolidate your understanding of a lecture. (Just pause in the middle or at the end for three minutes of fastwriting. It can save you hours of review.)

- a way to summarize your reading

Springboard 5: Fiction, Nonfiction, or Poetry?

Nonfiction is saying, "I caught a 12-inch fish." Fiction is saying, "I caught the biggest trout I ever saw before." In a lot of ways , fiction is more true than nonfiction.

—Gary Paulsen

Unlike botanists, writers have never organized their terminology into consistent classes, families, and species. Until they do, it's easiest to use the following simple definitions of fiction, nonfiction, and poetry:

- *Fiction*: Written works based on the writer's imagination. Fiction includes short stories, novels, plays, and any other piece of writing, except poems, in which the people, places and events of the story are created from the writer's imagination. The imaginary people in fiction are called characters, and the imaginary places are called settings. The imaginary events of a story make up the plot.

- *Nonfiction*: Written works based on either facts or opinions. Nonfiction is the biggest category of writing. Nonfiction includes essays, opinion pieces, magazine articles of all kinds, letters, histories, biographies, even cookbooks and dictionaries. Almost everything that is neither fiction nor poetry is nonfiction.

- *Poetry*: Poetry is the most personal of all writing. Poet A. E. Housman said "I could no more define poetry than a terrier can define a rat." But a terrier knows a rat when it sees one, and most people recognize a poem when they see one. A piece is a poem because the writer says it's a poem.

Try It

Choose any starting point and write down a fiction, nonfiction, and poetry idea for each. Writing ideas often come to mind in fiction or nonfiction form. Arbitrarily creating an idea for each category is one of the easiest ways to turn a starting point into a writing idea.

EXAMPLE

Starting Point—A paragraph about a blind dog named Alice (from "This is Your Life" filesheet, p. 8)

"Alice is blind. She carries her bowl around in her mouth when she wants food. She comes to work with me. Sometimes she waits in the shower or stands on my shoes in the morning when she wants me to hurry. She also snores. She can find her way out of any yard or building. The worst thing she ever did was dump a gallon-bottle of cooking oil on the living room rug."

Writing Ideas

Fiction: "My Dog Wears Purple Tennis Shoes," a story about Alice getting ready for work
Nonfiction: How to care for a blind dog
Poetry: A poem based on my feelings when Alice went blind

EXAMPLE

Starting Point—A computer (from a stop, look, and listen list)

Writing Ideas

Fiction: A story about a computer hacker who withdraws from the real world into a life centered on the machine
Nonfiction: Explanation of the uses of database programs for college students
Poetry: On masters and slaves in the information age

Springboard 6: The Genre Game

Outside of a dog books are man's best friend. Inside of a dog it's too dark to read.

—Groucho Marx

The word *genre* comes from the French word for *type*. It refers to similar pieces of writing. Used most often to refer to fiction, it applies to nonfiction as well.

Genres are not precise types. Genres develop because writers like a particular writer's work and use some of the themes or ideas in their own work. For example, the mystery genre was inspired by Wilkie Collins's novel *The Moonstone* and Sir Arthur Conan Doyle's Sherlock Holmes stories. So many writers have used this genre since then that subgenres ("the detective mystery," "the English mystery," "the adventure-mystery") are now developing. On the nonfiction side, the essay is the invention of one man, Michel de Montaigne, a seventeenth-century lawyer and eccentric who retired to a real ivy-covered tower to write his *Essays*. The word *essayer* means *to try* in French. Montaigne's notion was to use each essay to try one idea or one theme. Since then, the formal essay, the informal essay, the personal essay, the general academic essay, and specialized academic essays have developed as subgenres.

Before you begin, review the starter list of genres on the filesheet (pp. 15-16).

STARTER LIST OF GENRES (FILESHEET)

POPULAR FICTION GENRES

Nostalgia:	Stories based on memories of a character's past.
Tall Tale:	Exaggerated accounts of a real or imagined event.
Mystery:	Stories about solving a mystery.
Choose your own ending:	Stories written like a computer game where the reader chooses which paragraphs to read. (These stories are good practice for writing computer games.)
Adventure:	Stories showing characters overcoming danger.
Science fiction:	Stories set on imaginary planets, in imaginary societies, or in the future.
Fantasy:	Stories set in imaginary kingdoms or stories about mythical beasts or characters with special powers.
Horror:	Any kind of story designed to frighten or horrify.
Historical fiction:	Stories set in the real historical past with imaginary characters or plots.

POPULAR NONFICTION GENRES

Nostalgia:	Pieces based on memories of the writer.
Personal experience:	Pieces based on an event or problem in the lives of real people.
How-to:	Explanations of how to build, make, or operate things.
Self-help:	Pieces similar to how-to pieces, but based on helping people overcome personal problems like getting good grades or making friends. Self-help pieces don't emphasize step-by-step instructions as much as how-to's do.
Profile:	Pieces about an interesting person or group of people.
Consumer:	Tips on buying, selling, or repairing.
Opinion:	Pieces in which the writer expresses an opinion and makes a case for that point of view.
Information:	Straightforward presentations of facts new to the reader.
History:	Pieces which explain the history of people, places, things, or ideas.
Reporting:	Newspaper-style explanations of current events.

Collection: Collections of almost anything; for example, a dictionary is a collection of word definitions and spellings. A cookbook is a collection of recipes.

Biography: Life stories of interesting people.

Autobiography: The life story of the writer.

Essay: Pieces presenting, explaining, or arguing for one idea or theme. Subgenres are informal (often humorous), formal, personal, and academic.

Proposal: Pieces aimed at persuading others to provide money, time, or expertise for some project.

POETRY

There are only a few genres of poems; for example, Haiku or sonnets. Usually the poet wants to write a poem that is one of a kind, not part of a genre. However, poems can be based on memories, moods, observations, feelings, impressions, ideas, rhyme, or rhythm instead of a genre.

Try It

To play the genre game, write the names of the genres (and the things which inspire poems, if you wish) down the left hand side of a clean sheet of paper. Feel free to add genres from your own field of study to the genre list. Make up your own genre just for fun and add that.

Down the right hand side of the page, write down one writing idea for every genre. Don't worry about how good the ideas are, just try to come up with something. If you don't know very much about the starting point, it helps to write down the few things you do know before playing the game. When you are finished, put a check mark next to the ideas you like best. (See example below.)

EXAMPLE

Starting Point—Amazonian frog (from the "Stop, Look, and Listen List," p. 5)

Writing Ideas

FICTION GENRES	Writing Ideas List
Nostalgia:	*Summer of the Amazon*, a story of a boy's summer in the Amazon River Basin.
Tall Tale:	Story of a dinner where the guests are served frog legs to their distress. Title: *The Great Frog Leg Rebellion.*
Mystery:	Murder mystery where poison from an Amazonian frog skin is used as the murder weapon.
Romance:	Story of a biologist who falls in love with a woman reporter who has come to write an article on his work.
Choose your own ending:	Your spaceship has crashed on THE FROG PLANET (oops). What do you do next?
Adventure:	Tale of a fishing trip to Brazil that goes awry when one of the party tries to catch a frog.
Science fiction:	Life on a jungle planet.
Fantasy:	A story about a little boy whose pet frog can tell him the future.
Horror:	A story in which weird things happen every time the frogs start croaking.

Historical fiction: A story set in Brazil at the turn of the century

NONFICTION GENRES

Nostalgia: Memories of my father reading stories about places like the Amazon and dreaming of going there.

Personal experience: Frogs in the basement, a true tale.

How-to: How to care properly for laboratory frogs.

Self-help: Overcome your fear of frogs.

Profile: *The Man Who Loves Frogs*: story of a biologist who studies Amazonian frogs.

Consumer: Importing frogs is illegal! Ten tips to help consumers avoid buying endangered species.

Opinion: Why we should protect rare species.

Information: How the Indians of the Amazon are coping with the encroachment of modern civilization.

History: History of the discovery of a rare species in the Amazon.

Reporting: Reporting on the biology class study project on Amazonian frogs.

Collection: Frog leg cookbook.

Biography: Biography of the first anthropologist to work among the Amazonian Indians.

Autobiography: Why I have never been interested in frogs.

Essay: Comparing Amazonian frogs to North American frogs.

Proposal: Proposal to a faculty advisor to spend a term studying the adaptations of known frog species to different environments.

POETRY

memories: My father's voice reading Amazon tales.

observations: A poem called "Night Sounds."

feelings: My feelings when I read about faraway Brazil and frogs.

impressions: Impressions of a classroom with an Amazonian frog picture on the wall.

ideas: Even something as ugly as a frog can inspire us.

Springboard 7: Who, What, Why, When, Where, and How

> *I keep six honest serving men*
> *(They taught me all I knew)*
> *Their names are What and Why and When*
> *And How and Where and Who.*
>   —Rudyard Kipling

Following a simple, structured procedure can bring ideas to mind by giving one's imagination a little push to get going on its own. This springboard is especially useful for nonfiction ideas.

Try It

Get out your writing ideas notebook. Write down a starting point at the top of the page. Then write down a question about your starting point beginning with *who, what, why, when, where,* or *how.* Look at the question and try to write down two more questions or comments about your question.

Go back to your starting point and do the same thing over again. If you used *what* to write your first question, use *who, why, when, where,* or *how* for your next questions. Keep going until you have at least one question beginning with *who,* one beginning with *what,* and so forth. Note any writing ideas at the bottom of the page. Silly questions are encouraged.

EXAMPLE

Starting Point—freeway noise (from a stop, look, and listen list)

Questions

Where does the noise come from? the wheels or the car engines? bumps on the surface of the road?

What have people been doing to reduce noise from freeways? building fences? planting trees? tearing down old roads?

How does noise affect people? Can too much noise ruin your hearing? How much is too much? Are there any other health effects?

When is it noisest? at night? rush hour?

Who studies noise? engineers? doctors? Who else?

Why does noise exist? What makes sound? What stops sound? Is there any sound in space?

Writing Ideas

A research story about whether or not there is any sound in space and how the properties of sound are affected by a vacuum.

A report surveying the efforts of cities around the country to reduce freeway noise in urban areas.

EXAMPLE

Starting Point—a pencil (from a stop, look, and listen list)

Questions

How do they get the lead to go down the middle of the pencil? It's such a tight fit, you would think it grew that way. Do they have special machines to drill the holes?

When you plant a used pencil in the ground, will a new pencil grow? Do the pencil makers plant pencil seeds to grow new pencils?

Where are the pencil forests? Do they use leftover trees or big newly cut trees to make pencils? Maybe they glue scraps of wood together

What kind of trees make the best pencils? fir trees? pine trees? hardwoods?

Why do pencils always break or disappear just as you start to take a test or a phone message? Does somebody train them, or is it a pencil instinct? How come you never throw pencils away, but they never seem to be around when you need them. Where do they go?

Who invented the pencil? What inspired the inventor? Did the same person invent the pen?

Writing Ideas

The history of the lowly pencil.

A humorous essay on pencil behavior called "The Truth about Pencils."

An information piece explaining how pencils are made.

Springboard 8: People, Places, and Problems

Whatever pulls you to it like a secret magnet may be your story meat.
Your imagination is a mysterious and somewhat holy place.
                                                                    —Paul Darcy Boles

This springboard is the fiction equivalent of "Who, What, Why, When, Where, and How." It is based on arbitrarily inventing a character, a setting, and a problem for the character to solve.

Try It

Set up a piece of paper with four headings across the top: *Starting Point, Person* (*Character*), *Place* (or *Setting*), and *Problem* (or *Central Conflict*). To play the game, think up a starting point, person, a place, and a problem that person wants or needs to solve. Let the starting point suggest people, places, or problems, or just make them up from thin air. Give the person a name, if you haven't already. Then write, "This is a story about a _____, named _____ who _____ _____." Just fill in the blanks.

EXAMPLE

Starting Point	*Person*	*Place*	*Problem*
desk	a boy	sitting at desk	lost homework

This is a story about a boy, named Jim, who is always losing his assignments and has just discovered that he has lost his social studies homework for the third time in a row....

EXAMPLE

Starting Point	*Person*	*Place*	*Problem*
siren	elderly lady	house near hospital	hates sirens

This is a story about an elderly lady, named Florence, who lived in London during this blitz and can't stand sirens....

EXAMPLE

Starting Point	*Person*	*Place*	*Problem*
pages ruffling	librarian	sailboat	bored

This is a story about a librarian, named Jack, who is bored with his job and wants adventure. One day on his way to work, he is attracted by an advertisement seeking a cook for a sailboat going on a race around the world....

EXAMPLE

Starting Point	*Person*	*Place*	*Problem*
"This school is a mess"	girl	Planet Xenon	a tidy person on a messy planet

This is a story about a student, named Jeso, who goes away to a school on the planet Xenon and is disgusted that the school — and everything else — is a mess because Xenonites don't care about litter. So she goes on a crusade to change their ways....

Springboard 9: Wacko

What happens to the hole when the cheese is gone?
—Bertolt Brecht

Wacko is so named because the wackier your mood, the more fun it is. Frankly, Wacko is fun even when you aren't looking for writing ideas. This is a great group game that calls for a certain amount of inspired lunacy.

Keep in mind that writing ideas sometimes come to mind in complete paragraphs or sentences. If your idea arrives whole-cloth, don't wait! Get busy and put it on paper before it disappears.

Try It

Get out your writing ideas notebook. Choose an item from any of your lists of starting points that is a fact, an opinion, or an observation. Then make it go wacko by turning the idea upside down or changing it around. Let your first wacky idea lead to others and keep going until you run dry. One of our wacky ideas just might turn out to be a good writing idea.

EXAMPLE

Starting Point—"I hate zucchini." (from "This is Your Life," p. 8)

Wacky Ideas

Suppose I liked zucchini. Suppose zucchini liked me! Could zucchinis be trying to get my attention? Is that why they grow to forty pounds overnight if I fail to pick them each evening? Is that why zucchinis appear on my doorstep or my desk when I'm not looking?

Writing Idea

A humorous essay called *The Zucchini Conspiracy* about what zucchinis really do when people aren't looking.

EXAMPLE

Starting Point—"From all levels of government, federal, state, and local, Americans get 150,000 new laws and 2 million new regulations every year." (Isaac Asimov, *Book of Facts*, p. 197)

Wacky Ideas

Suppose a country could only pass one law each year. What law would people choose? Most people would probably choose "love thy neighbor" as the best law. Would it work? Maybe not.

Writing Idea

A fictional newspaper article from *The National Snoop*, (Anywhere, U.S.A.)

Mr. Jake Blunt, owner of the Flat Earth Deli and Gas Station, was hauled into Superior Court today and charged with two counts of Not Loving Thy Neighbor. Blunt allegedly snarled at his neighbor on two separate occasions for not returning Blunt's lawnmower. Blunt was found guilty on both counts and paid a $100.00 fine.

"There oughta be a law," growled Blunt at reporters afterwards. Reporters reminded him that there was a law: "Love thy neighbor."

"Yeah?" replied Blunt. "Well it's not all it's cracked up to be."

Notes from the Pros:
On Falling in Love and Burning Out

Writing begins with passion: passion for the subject; passion for the genre; passion for the ideas. Passion is the engine that drives writing. Without it, writers cannot sustain the energy to finish. Writers who work on contracts specifying the same genres and the same subjects over and over burn out. Sir Arthur Conan Doyle killed Sherlock Holmes just to escape from the genre and the character. Other writers have stopped writing altogether. The wise ones went back to the beginning and started with a genre and a theme of their own choosing—with a passion.

Students don't begin to really learn to write until they fall in love with a story, a genre, a subject, or an idea and write about it wholeheartedly. It's a great moment. Unfortunately, most students never discover it because schools often have the process backward. Students are assigned "papers" on specified topics over, and over, and over. They burn out before they ever fall in love.

If you want to turn on to writing, remember that passion comes first. Choose what to write about and how to write it over and over. Don't save creative writing until later. Creative writing *is* writing; you need to discover that passion before you will improve. Keep moving on: try new genres, new subjects, and new ideas. Learn terms and techniques one day; write without direction the next. Do some practice pieces, some complete pieces. Even when you work on school assignments, try to start with an intriguing argument or a fascinating fact. Above all, avoid burning out. Then, with time, you will fall in love.

Student's Notebook:
On Procrastination

Procrastination plagues all writers and causes more writing failures than any other problem. Professionals soon learn to build their work habits to counter the procrastination pest before it ever gets established. Here are a few strategies that you can use if you tend to delay writing until the day before the deadline.

1. *Start work immediately*

   Projects look less daunting from the inside than from the outside, so get into the work as fast as possible. Spend five minutes on any of the springboards in the first three chapters of this book and another fifteen minutes writing on the topic in your practice journal. Do this as soon as you receive an assignment or decide on a writing project. Once you make a start, you will have momentum on your side. Keep building that momentum by working a little at a time.

2. *Make up a writing schedule with intermediate deadlines.*

   Most professional writers plan to spend one-third of their time prewriting (getting ideas and planning), one-third drafting, and one-third editing (revising and polishing). Setting deadlines for finishing prewriting, drafting, and editing breaks the project into manageable phases and allows you to check your progress before the crisis arrives.

3. *Set up a daily or weekly goal.*

   Beginners panic over the final deadline; professionals panic over a daily goal. Take a tip from the professionals and set aside regular time in your schedule for writing projects. Give yourself a reasonable goal for each session. You may not be able to set aside time for writing every day, but you should set aside time every week. Professionals set a reasonable goal: so many pages per day or week. If they miss the goal one day, they make it up the next. Get in the writing habit. If you don't use your writing time for work-in-progress, use it for practice. Nothing defeats procrastination like a well-established habit.

4. *Find out why you are tempted and take steps.*

   Most people procrastinate writing because they worry that the piece won't turn out well, they feel uncomfortable or unfamiliar with the subject, or they simply feel exposed by writing thoughts on paper. List your reasons objectively, but don't ignore them. Make a plan to deal with them. it can be as simple as finding a friend to read and discuss your drafts, devising a research plan, or discussing an outline or a writing idea with your professor.

   Watch out for false reasons. You may need to restock your kitchen cupboard, finish other assignments, or take your cat to the vet, but do you really need to do it during your writing time? Procrastination can sneak up on you. Reasons that sound perfectly sensible as you put off writing will sound like flimsy excuses once the deadline looms large. Get tough. Set aside time for writing projects and fiercely defend it.

Chapter 2

Planning

Plans will get you into things but you got to work your way out.
— Will Rogers

INTRODUCTION

When most people think of writing plans, they think of an outline. English teachers faithfully teach the outline and usually ask students to turn it in with the finished piece. If asked, students admit that they usually write their outlines after finishing the drafts. There is nothing wrong with this. Outlines are excellent revision tools. The problem with outlines is that they don't help the novice get started writing. And starting a piece of writing feels like pinning clouds to a bulletin board. It's hard to know what to tack down first. Everyone asks the same questions: How can I research before I know what I am going to say? How do I know what to say until I outline? How can I outline until I know what I research?

It's difficult to advise the beginning writer how to proceed. Nowhere are experienced writers less consistent than in preparing to write. They talk about it; they refuse to talk about it. They make outlines; they hate them. They write 70,000 word summaries; they try to find just one word. They barely research; they collect volumes. They start drafting from the beginning and write to the end; they won't start drafting until they finish the last page. They plan little by little between drafting sessions; they plan everything before they begin. They call what they do before they write by a thousand different names: planning, outlining, research, narrowing the topic, finding a slant, preliminary drafts, prewriting, or incubating. Every writer and every piece is different — not a reassuring or helpful thought for a beginner wondering what to do next with a handful of clouds.

Planning is not just a matter of organization. On the contrary, many writers find it easier to clean up the organization when they revise. But all writers and especially inexperienced writers need to plan because writing well demands confidence. If you feel unsure of your facts or tentative about your point of view, the piece will suffer and so will you. In order to sound crisp, clear, and authoritative, you need to feel in command of the material. Planning is your opportunity to take charge, to build confidence, to lay a foundation to support yourself once you start writing.

You can approach planning any way you think best. What helps others may not help you, and what works well for one piece may not work for the next. Most of the time, however, the easiest approach is to go step-by-step through the corners of the writing triangle, planning whatever you need for each corner.

The Writing Idea Triangle Revisited

As you can see from the illustration, we fudged on the names of the point of the triangle in Chapter 1. They are really *Background, Focus,* and *Order.* The *Background* corner of the triangle covers researching the subject for nonfiction pieces and researching the setting and the characters' backgrounds for fiction. The *Focus* corner of the triangle consists of a series of crucial decisions you make about how to handle the piece. The *Order* corner of the triangle covers any choices you make about what to cover first, second, and third.

BACKGROUND

(Subject)

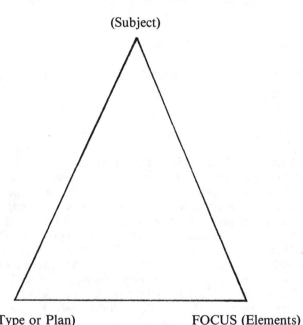

ORDER (Type or Plan)   FOCUS (Elements)

	Nonfiction	*Fiction*
	Ideal Reader	Characters
Category, genre,	Purpose	Setting
outline or rough draft	Mood	Narrator
	Key idea	Central Conflict

When you plan, you can begin at any corner of the triangle, but most people find it easiest to start with the focus, then research the background, and finally develop the order. For this reason, this chapter is broken into three sections:

"Finding a Focus," "Background Research," and "Finding an Order." The springboards are designed either to help you get your planning started or to give you a variety of approaches you can use to do your own planning. The only ones that we recommend doing with every piece you plan are those in the first section on finding a focus. After that, you can pick and choose the springboards which most appeal to you.

FINDING A FOCUS

Writers make many decisions before they write. The prewriting choices critical to finding a focus are:

Nonfiction	Fiction
Ideal Reader	Characters
Purpose	Setting
Mood	Narrator
Key idea	Central conflict

These choices, or focus points, have two things in common. First, each choice *must* be made. Every writer makes them consciously or makes them unconsciously. Second, accidentally changing even one of them in the middle of the draft will *always* result in a major rewrite or a confusing disaster. These choices serve as focus points because they operate a bit like the visual artist's horizon line and perspective points. They aren't terribly difficult choices to make, but making them aligns the perspective of the rest of the work. That's why making them deliberately in advance pulls the piece into sharp focus but changing them mid-draft distorts the focus, ending in confusion. If we have one piece of advice to offer you, it is to deliberately make these choices for every piece you write, then stick to them all the way through the draft. Following this rule will contribute more to your success than any other planning you do.

Springboard 1: Focus Points for Nonfiction

i never think at all when i write / nobody can do two things at the same time / and do them both well
—Don Marquis

There is an old saying among writers: "Nonfiction starts hard and ends easy; fiction starts easy and ends hard." Stories can just grow from what happens first and what happens next. That rarely happens in nonfiction. A clear focus wins 90 percent of the nonfiction battle. Choosing the ideal reader, purpose, mood, and key idea helps most people start more easily. Put careful thought into these choices. Nonfiction is especially sensitive to changes of reader or mood. As you research and outline, you can refine these choices or change them; just don't change them once you start writing unless you are reconciled to a complete rewrite.

Try It

Choose a writing idea or any nonfiction subject. Read the explanations and tips on each choice on the filesheet (p. 30), then fill out the checklist at the end in pencil, so that you can change it. Write a sample paragraph or two in your practice journal using your first set of choices, then change one or more of your choices and write another sample. After sampling a few options, choose the ones you like best.

NONFICTION FOCUS POINTS (FILESHEET)

1. IDEAL READER. Who will read the piece? Thinking of one particular person as you write helps you decide what to say. Suppose you use "how to use a word processing program" as your writing idea. You would say one thing to a fourteen-year-old, who has little experience with writing but enjoys computers, something completely different to an older writer, who knows about writing but may feel anxious about computers.

   You can choose a real person or create an imaginary one, but try to choose someone who knows less about your subject than you; for example, someone younger than you or someone learning about your subject for the first time. *Don't choose your professor.* You will keep wondering what to say that the professor doesn't already know. View professors as helpful editors, not as readers. It helps. If you must choose an expert for an ideal reader, plan your research so that you will know more than your ideal reader before you start planning.

2. PURPOSE. Why are you writing this piece? Why would your ideal reader want to read it? Do you want to entertain your reader? show your reader how to do something? persuade your reader to do something? describe something your reader hasn't seen? Answer these questions, and you will know your purpose.

   Think of your writing as a gift. You give your gift to your ideal reader. *Your purpose is what you plan to give.*

EXAMPLES

- to *entertain* my ideal reader

- to *show* my ideal reader *how something works*

- to *show* my ideal reader *how to* do something

- to *persuade* my ideal reader to do something

- to *report* what happened to my ideal reader

- to *give my opinion* on something to my ideal reader

- to *explain* to my ideal reader *why* I have an opinion

- to *describe* something to my ideal reader

- to *trace the history* of something for my ideal reader

- to *show* my ideal reader *why* (or *how*) *two things are the same*

- to *show* my ideal reader *why* (or *how*) *two things are different*

You can also have two purposes, for example, "to explain how to do something in an entertaining way," "to give my opinion and explain why," or "to describe something and trace its history."

3.   MOOD. Like a good conversation, a piece of writing shares a mood as well as ideas. You can be friendly and helpful. You can go on a crusade for your ideas. You can be detached and logical. You can be funny and informal. Think of sitting down with your ideal reader over lunch and talking with him or her about your writing idea. What kind of mood do you want your conversation to have? (If you are writing academic papers, keep in mind that the major difference between academic writing and other types of writing is its detached, thorough mood.)

EXAMPLES

humorous	informative	silly
crusading	ironic	angry
friendly	helpful	detached
leisurely	quick	commanding
critical	serious	sad
thorough	argumentative	peaceful
whimsical	outrageous	even-handed
provoking	compassionate	energetic

4.   KEY IDEA. Your key idea is your writing idea. Any article, essay, or book should be about just one key idea tying everything else together. To choose your key idea, either copy down your original writing idea or use your decisions about the ideal reader, purpose, and mood to sharpen it up. The sharper your idea, the easier it is to write nonfiction.

EXAMPLES

Original Writing Idea: How to use a word processing program.

Key Ideas: How to learn a word processing program in no time flat

How to use a word processing program for the first time.

How to use a word processing program to create mailing lists.

A day in the life of a writer with a word processor.

Using a word processor to enhance your creativity.

Original Writing Idea: What freedom means to me.

Key Ideas: Freedom means rights *and* responsibilities.

Freedom must be practiced every day.

Freedom is enjoying the little things in life.

Freedom is having dreams of your own.

A story of one person's escape to freedom.

Original Writing Idea: Getting good grades.

Key Ideas: Why students want good grades.

A survey of professors on their grading practices.

Ten tips for getting better grades.

What to do when you get a poor grade.

The history of grading in American public schools and how it shapes today's practices.

Do grades help students learn?

Sharpening up your key idea takes a little practice. Sometimes it helps to pretend that you are holding a camera. Suppose your subject is trees. Are you going to talk about the big wide-angle picture, panning back to show the whole forest and perhaps, trace its history? Or are you going to use a narrow lens and focus on the story of just one tree in that forest? Perhaps you'll tell the story of something in between—of one type of tree in that forest or of all the trees along one stream.

Think, too, about the time period. If you are going to discuss one tree, are you going to cover its whole history going back to the Ice Age? Or are you going to show what happens in and around that tree during spring, summer, fall, and winter? What about just one day in the life of that tree?

It sometimes helps to try to think of several key ideas that might work, then choose the best one. Remember to *choose just one key idea.* You can only tell one story at a time. Two will turn out to be confusing and very hard to write.

NONFICTION FOCUS POINTS (CHECKLIST)

My writing idea is: _____

_____ .

1. IDEAL READER
My ideal reader is: _____ .

I chose this ideal reader because: _____

_____

_____ .

2. PURPOSE
The purpose of this piece is to: _____

_____

_____ .

My ideal reader would like to read this because: _____

_____

_____ .

3. MOOD
The mood of this piece is: _____

_____ .

4. KEY IDEA
My key idea is:_____

_____

_____ .

Springboard 2: Focus Points for Fiction

Why shouldn't *truth be stranger than fiction? Fiction, after all, has to make sense.*

—Mark Twain

Although you write more nonfiction in college than fiction, we have not excluded fiction from this book because writing fiction, apart from the sheer fun of it, improves your writing. Fiction lets you be yourself. You can explore your style, tackle themes that intrigue you, use a large range of sentences, and stretch your vocabulary. Whereas nonfiction improves your fiction by teaching you structure and brevity, fiction enriches your nonfiction by teaching you description and sparkle.

You may prefer fiction or nonfiction, but try a little of each. Try different genres. Each genre puts different demands on a writer; for example, action stories demand skill at building suspense. Nostalgic stories stress describing settings and characters to build a mood. All fiction puts ruthless demands on your logic. The real world may not make much sense at times; fictional worlds must always make sense. If your science fiction setting has no gravity, characters can never drop cups of coffee on the floor. Meeting each of these challenges builds your writing skill in some way. The things you learn from each different type of writing you try can be applied to everything you write.

Try It

Choose a writing idea or any fictional character or setting. Read the explanations and tips for each choice on the filesheet below, then fill out the checklist at the end in pencil, so that you can change it. Write a sample paragraph or two in your practice journal using your first set of choices, then change one or more of your choices and write another sample. After sampling a few options, choose the ones you like best.

FICTION FOCUS POINTS (FILESHEET)

1. CHARACTERS

Stories are about characters. A good plot with dull, flat characters won't satisfy your reader, but even a thin plot can carry a story with great characters. Always start with your characters, then worry about what happens to them.

The Main Character

The most important character in your story is called the *main character*. You can only have *one* main character. The main character has a problem to solve, wants something, or tries to do something. This is called the central conflict. To use simple examples everyone recognizes, Dorothy, the main character in the *Wizard of Oz* wants to get home to Kansas. In the Sherlock Holmes stories, Holmes wants to solve the mystery. Your first prewriting decision is to choose your main character. What does your main character want? That's your central conflict.

The Secondary Characters

The *secondary characters* are the other important characters besides the main character. For example, Tin Man, Scarecrow, and Lion are secondary characters in the *Wizard of Oz*. Dr. Watson of the Sherlock Holmes stories is also a secondary character, even though he is vital to the stories. The difference between the secondary characters and the main character is that the central conflict belongs to the main character. Tin Man, Scarecrow, and Lion help Dorothy get to Kansas. They just happen to solve some of their own problems along the way.

You can choose just one or two secondary character or a whole crowd of them. You don't need to have a secondary character, but, if you choose more than one or two, be careful not to have too many. One or two is usually more than enough to make a good story.

Minor Character and Bit Players

There are two other types of characters that you should know about, although you don't need to make any decisions about them right away. You can make them up as you write. These are *minor characters* and *bit players*.

Minor characters usually have names. The reader learns a little bit about them, but not much. For example, the wizard and all the witches in the *Wizard of Oz* are minor characters. Sherlock's clients are minor characters. Villains are often minor characters.

Bit players, on the other hand, are hardly people at all. They do their little bit for the story and disappear. They open the gates to Oz, drive taxis to the airport, answer questions at hotel desks. They usually don't even have names.

You can think of your main and secondary characters as round characters. The reader knows all about them in detail. They are rounded out. The minor characters and bit characters are flat. Your reader never learns very much about them; they are just there to move the story forward in some way.

2. THE CENTRAL CONFLICT

The central conflict is your main character's biggest problem. It's easiest to think of a central conflict by asking yourself, "What does my main character want? Does he or she want to do something? solve a problem? get something? make something?" That's your central conflict. When your main character gets what he or she wants, your story ends. (Sometimes your main character doesn't get what he or she wants. The story ends once it's clear that the main character will never get it.)

Beginners often make the mistake of creating several central conflicts. Stick to just one. Just because you choose one central conflict doesn't mean there won't be plenty of other problems for your characters to solve. Dorothy didn't make it home to Kansas without bumping against witches and dark forests. Secondary characters have their problems, too. Tin Man wanted a heart, and Scarecrow wanted a brain. But the central conflict, the problem that started everything else, that drove the story from start to finish, was Dorothy's desire to go home.

Think of your story as a series of stair steps building up to a high point. Each step forward is another step to resolving the central conflict, but each step also has complications or setbacks to overcome. The story builds up to a final, big setback—a crisis. All seems lost. Then the main character overcomes the last setback, the central conflict is resolved, and the story quickly ends.

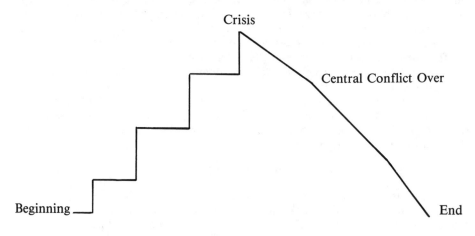

Because you know that the story ends once the central conflict is resolved, it may help you to decide how the story will end first. Then decide what the crisis point will be, and last of all, decide how to begin.

3. SETTING

The setting is where your story takes place. Unless you are writing science fiction, it is usually best to choose settings that you have experienced first-hand for your first few stories. Your setting has a lot to do with the atmosphere of the story, and lack of familiarity with the setting deprives you of vital details you need to evoke the feeling of that place.

You can choose as many settings as you wish, but keep it simple. More than two or three major setting changes may become confusing. You'll spend more time moving people from one place to another than you will telling the story. If you have more than one, it sometimes helps to think in terms of big settings and little ones. The big setting might be a town. The little ones might be the school, the local hardware store, or the town square. Your big setting might be a country, the little ones a city in that country, a small town in the mountains, or a roadside cafe on a main highway.

How important is setting to your story? If your story is set in an unfamiliar place, such as another planet or a far-off country, the setting might be as critical to the story as the main character. If the setting is uninteresting or does not help build an atmosphere, the setting may matter little. Make this decision now. It will affect how much research you do on the setting.

4. NARRATOR

You have one more imaginary person to create before starting your story—the narrator. The narrator is the person who tells the story. Readers like to pretend that stories really happened. As they read, they feel almost like they are listening to stories around the campfire, and they want to know why the person telling the story knows what happened. Is the narrator a character in the story and knows about it because he or she was there? Or is the narrator someone who found out about it and is retelling it?

If your narrator is a character from the story, the narrator will use *I* to tell the story. This is called a *first-person narrator*. (e.g., "*I* walked the dog and then went to the store."—the narrator is a character named Mary in the story.) If your narrator is not a character in the story, the narrator will tell the story using *he, she,* or *they*. This is called a *third-person narrator*. (e.g., "*Mary* walked the dog, and then went to the store.") The third-person narrator is sometimes called the omniscient or all-knowing narrator. The omniscient narrator knows what every character did and thought as if the story was pieced together by speaking to all the characters after it was over.

First person narrators are often easiest for beginners. Be aware, however, that you may encounter problems when the narrator can't participate in something that needs to be described to the reader. You will learn how to handle these tricky problems when you bump into them. ("Little did I know as I sunned on the beach that Sam the Evil was at that very moment planning my untimely death...") The next time you read a first person story, notice how other writers handle this problem. Be sure to avoid choosing a first person narrator who is killed in the story. Of course, you can say that this book was a diary found in the dead person's effects, but why resort to a hokey cliché like that when you can simply choose a narrator who lives to tell the tale?

The tricky part of the omniscient, third-person narator is that, even though your narrator knows everything, you must still maintain a clear point of view. To do this, you must write as though you were looking at the story through the eyes of one person most of the time. Novelists may change point of view, but point of view changes easily confuse readers and must be done carefully. Short story writers circumvent this problem by sticking to one point of view. The first time you try the third person narrator, you may find it easiest to write the rough draft in first person and then convert to third person.

Choose whichever narrator you like, but stick with the same narrator all the way through the story.

One final tip: have your narrator tell the story in past tense (e.g., "Mary *went* to the store," not "Mary *goes* to the store"). The easiest way to do this naturally is to pretend that your narrator is telling the story after the story is over, not as it happens. Without going into details, take our word for it: present tense fiction is especially hard to write.

5. STORY STATEMENT

The last step to your prewriting choices is to write a story statement describing the story in a sentence or two. This is not a requirement, but it helps most people maintain a clear sense of the story—something that may otherwise get lost once you are enmeshed in writing individual scenes.

FICTION FOCUS POINTS CHECKLIST

My writing idea is: _____

_____ .

1. CHARACTERS

The name of my main character is (first, middle, and last) _____

_____ .

My main character wants: _____

_____ .

The names of my secondary characters are:

_____   _____

_____   _____

_____   _____

2. CENTRAL CONFLICT

The central conflict of my story is: _____

_____ .

The story ends when: _____

_____ .

The crisis comes when: _____

_____ .

The story begins when: _____

_____ .

3. SETTING(S)

My story is set in (name the big setting or settings): _____

_____

_____ .

List possible little settings within the big setting(s):_____

_____

_____

The setting is _____ important _____ not important.

4. NARRATOR

My (first person) narrator is the character in my story named: _____

_____ .

My (third person) narrator is a person outside the story who is retelling it _____.

5. STORY STATEMENT – This is a story about: _____

_____

_____ .

Notes from the Pros:
On Writing to Length

Writing a specified number of words or pages is one of the most difficult aspects of writing. The natural length of a story or of a nonfiction piece is a product of the prewriting choices and the author's style. A change of one prewriting choice will change the length. An article on how to clean a carburetor aimed at mechanics is likely to be much shorter than the same article aimed at people who don't know what a carburetor is. With so many variables, it takes writers years—and plenty of editing—to be able to write a piece to an approximate length. Even then, they often make mistakes and must rewrite the entire piece. The shorter the piece, the harder it is to write to a specified length.

Curiously, the best way to learn to write to length is to avoid thinking about length at all. Concentrate on making your points briefly and clearly. Over time you will develop a feel for the types of prewriting choices that produce a particular length, and you will find that you can say more with fewer words. You will develop more control over the length if you follow the standard rule, "Write long, then cut by a third." Most important, never pad your work.

Running wildly over or under length most often results from a loose, ill-defined, or inappropriate key idea. When cutting doesn't work, revise your key idea and try again.

Unlike publishers, who assign lengths to meet space or financial limitations, professors are much less concerned about length. As long as the paper is clear, organized, and responds to the assignment, few professors care about running a few pages over or under the assigned length. Students worry too much about it, as one professor accidentally discovered when he jokingly assigned 984 words, then got back ten papers of exactly 984 words. If questions of length tend to bother you, despite our advice, try thinking of lengths not as a certain number of words or pages, but as a category, such as a vignette or an article. Below is a list of the categories used in the publishing industry along with the approximate length publishers expect for those categories:

FICTION LENGTH CATEGORIES

Category	Definition	Approximate Length
scene	a segment of a story	500-2,000 words
chapter	a section of a novel	1,500-7,500 words
vignette	a very short, but complete story	500-2,000 words
short story	a complete story, generally told from one viewpoint	1,500-7,000 words
novelette	a short novel	7,000-50,000 words
novel	a complete story told in several chapters, often from multiple viewpoints	50,000-150,000 words

NONFICTION LENGTH CATEGORIES

Category	Definition	Approximate Length
section	a segment of a nonfiction piece	100-1,500 words
chapter	a segment of a nonfiction book	1,500-7,000 words
filler (sometimes called a short essay, short article, or anecdote)	a very short, but complete piece	100-1,500 words
article (also called a short piece or short essay)	a complete piece of nonfiction on one aspect of a theme or topic	1,500-7,500 words
book	a complete piece covering several aspects of a theme	30,000-120,000 words
reference	a collection of information on a particular subject organized according to a pattern	no limits

In the world of the working writer, lengths are subject to publishing fads. The short story was king at the turn of the century, and 7,000 words was the most popular length. By World War II, the average length of the short story dropped to 3,000 words. Many short story writers found themselves unable to write to that length. Some abandoned the short story and turned to novels; others abandoned writing altogether.

Student's Notebook: On Analyzing Assignments

Anytime you write on assignment, you must meet not only your own expectations but also those of the person giving the assignment. Meeting other people's expectations can be frustrating and sometimes frightening. You can save yourself both time and anxiety by analyzing the assignment and clarifying those expectations early. Don't be afraid to share your analysis with your professor or your boss to make sure you understand what he or she wants. You are not wasting time. On the contrary, it's much easier to get you started on the right track than to help you untangle a work well underway.

Anytime you write pieces for another person, be they term papers for professors, reports and proposals for bosses, or articles for publishers, do some preliminary analysis and, if necessary, set up an appointment to discuss your plans before you go too far. Of course, the things that you need to clarify will vary with the assignment, but the five points (pp. 42-43) usually cover the necessary expectation for most assignments.

1. *Why am I doing this?*

   Professors don't read 150 papers on a sunny weekend for fun; bosses don't assign reports as meaningless busy work. They have a purpose for giving the assignment. Your professor may want to give you an opportunity to consolidate what you have learned by writing about it, give you the time to do independent research, or give you a chance to try a particular genre or format. Your boss may need your report in order to report to his or her boss or may just want to give you a way to present some of your ideas. You stand a much better chance of producing satisfactory work if you understand the reason for it. The next time you get an assignment, instead of asking "how long should it be?" or "when is it due?", try asking what the professor hopes students will learn from the assignment or what your boss needs from your report.

2. *Are my prewriting choices appropriate?*

   In theory the prewriting choices are up to you. In practice, teachers, bosses, and publishers expect you to make appropriate choices to suit their needs. The magazine publisher's ideal reader is the person who typically buys the magazine. No matter how good your work, the publisher will reject pieces written for the wrong ideal reader. Professors and bosses expect particular choices of ideal readers, purposes, or moods as well. At the very least, they expect those choices to be within an acceptable range.

   Unfortunately, even experienced publishers may not state their expectations clearly. It's up to you to make sure your choices are appropriate. One successful technical writer cut the writing time for her department in half by insisting that top management agree to the ideal reader and purpose before the writing staff started work. You, too, can cut your work time in half by making your choices, then checking them out when you discuss your plans.

3. *Is my key idea workable?*

   A professor or a boss may not have time to review a rough draft in order to make suggestions, but they can help you decide if your key idea makes sense, needs tightening, or may get you into deep water. Once you agree upon a workable key idea, they can save you hundreds of hours of research by suggesting books, articles, or people to consult. Most professors are happy to help serious students who respect their expertise. Bosses, too, appreciate being treated as expert resources.

4. *Can I see an example?*

   One good example beats a thousand explanations or comments. If you don't have a good example, ask for one or find one on your own and ask if it is a good one. Study the prewriting choices used for the example: who was the ideal reader? what was the purpose and mood? Outline it. Read it aloud. If you can find two good examples, compare them. Just getting a feel for the example will help you as much as anything you do—especially if you are working with a person for the first time, with a new genre, or in an unfamiliar subject area.

5. *Will you review a sample?*

For long pieces or pieces where it is vital that you do it the way the other person wants it, reviewing a sample can save everyone time. Turn in a sample chapter, the first page, or the most important section, then go over the comments before you write the rest of the piece. This works especially well when you write for a group of people. Nothing is more demoralizing than watching five people pick your hard-won rough draft to pieces. Let the group pick apart the sample, then write the rest of it alone, in peace, keeping their comments in mind. You will produce better work in about half the time.

Student's Notebook:
On Writing Terms

When you learn terms such as *character, fiction,* and *ideal reader,* you not only learn what choices to make but also have some way to talk about your writing. Just knowing that there are such things as *genres, settings, dialogue, action,* and *examples* inspires writing. Understanding what a *scene* is or what a *section* is helps you organize your work.

Learning writing necessarily involves learning terminology, but there are some significant problems with writing jargon. First of all, writing terms are vague and don't hold up to precise definition. Most represent a decision made by writers, for good or ill. A sentence is anything the writer starts with a capital letter and ends with a period. It's impossible to be more specific. Not all sentences have a subject and a verb or represent a unified thought. Even run-on and incomplete sentences are still sentences. Second, no two writers, teachers, or editors use the same terms. They might call the ideal reader the *audience,* the *reader,* or the *market.* They might call the key idea the *slant, angle, purpose, topic, subject, narrowed topic,* or *subject,* or the *lead.* They might call the first sentence or the first few paragraphs the *lead,* the *opening,* the *hook,* or the *thesis.* Finally, fiction and nonfiction writers need to know different terms. Literary critics use overlapping terms with a different emphasis. Discussing grammar or punctuation requires a set of terms aimed at dissecting sentences, useful only in the final stages of polishing.

Some writing teachers don't formally teach terms. They bring them up naturally during editing sessions and class discussion, so that students gradually learn some terms on their own. You may be better off speeding up the process and learning a few vital terms on your own, so that you have a base with which to discuss your writing.

Start with *categories* and *genres,* the *prewriting choices, scenes* and *sections,* and at least some of the techniques in chapter 4, such as *action, dialogue, examples,* and *anecdotes.* After these, choose any terms that you find helpful or inspiring. Learn grammar and punctuation terms separate from writing terms.

To overcome the circular definition problem, use the same steps to learn every important term:

1. Define the term *briefly* and read several examples. Getting a feel for examples is more important than memorizing definitions.

2. Try it in your practice journal. (Three to five minutes—no more or you will bog down.)

3. Store some kind of follow-up literature with your practice journal. The filesheets in this book are designed for this. A page of notes will work as well. The point is to store a brief reminder of the things you want to learn in a convenient spot. Just reading through these briefs will inspire your writing.

BACKGROUND RESEARCH

Ideas, research, organization, and style—each plays a part in a writer's success. But a writer wandering through the bookstore with a little spare change is likely to go home with a book on research. A beautiful style, an elegant structure, or a clever plot won't satisfy a reader starved for facts or authentic detail. The path to those facts and details is research. Professionals may devote as much as 40 percent of their time to it.

Of course, the word *research* means different things to different writers. The nonfiction writer wants to find facts, examples, and anecdotes—the bricks and mortar of nonfiction. Fiction writers research their characters' lives and the story settings in order to write with realism and authenticity. The author with a computer programmer as a main character needs to know something about computer programming. Readers won't believe a snowstorm in Rio de Janeiro or a dust storm in Seattle unless the writer mentions documented snowstorms or dust storms in those places.

Professional writers don't research solely to find facts or realistic details. They research because they know that few things are more painful than writing when you are unsure of the facts or vague on the details, but research builds confidence. They keep researching until they feel in command, until their words flow onto paper naturally with the crisp, clear voice of an expert even though they use only a tenth of their research in the final piece. Research makes good writing, but it also makes putting words on paper a pleasure.

There are four basic ways to approach research: library research; interviews with experts, participants, or eye witnesses; direct observation; and experiments. The approach you choose depends on the piece, your access to sources, your time, and your budget. You can fly to Rio to observe the setting directly or you can read a good book on Brazil. In truth, each different approach is a little art in itself. The activities in this section will help you get started; you can improve your abilities by reading detailed books on the particular approach you choose. Before you launch into studying how to conduct interviews or tackle a library, give some thought to your major. If you are majoring in history or literature, you will probably get the most from your time by studying library research. Journalism majors should start with interviews, while engineering, social science, and fiction majors would do well to begin with direct observation. Investing a little time in learning the art of research now will save plenty of research time later on. Below are some good introductory books.

Research Made Easy: A Guide for Students and Writers by Robert Matzen gives you a quick tour of the basics. *Knowing Where to Look: The Ultimate Guide to Research* by Lois Horowitz will turn you into a super efficient library whiz. *The Craft of Interviewing* by John Brady is the dog-eared companion to many a writer. No serious writing student should be without it. *Doing Your Own Research: How to do Basic Descriptive Research in the Social Sciences and Humanities* by Eileen Kane will introduce you to direct observation. Fiction writers should read *Look, Think, and Write* by Hart Day Leavit and David Sohn. Although not a book on research per se, it introduces fiction writers to writing from direct, detailed observation which comprises the bulk of "research" for fiction writing.

The activities in this section of the planning chapter were designed to help you get started. The first is a simple way to break the research into manageable chunks; the second helps you with your first day in the library, and the third helps fiction writers develop the lives of their characters.

Springboard 3: Breaking Down the Problem

Everybody is ignorant, only on different subjects.
— Will Rogers

The most common problem students have with research is not knowing where to begin. This activity will help you break your research problem into bite-sized chunks, so that you can develop a little game plan to guide you once you reach the library.

Try It

There are four steps to making up your game plan:

1. Break your story statement or key idea into areas to study.

2. Make a list of "pointers" for each area.

3. List potential sources.

4. Choose priorities.

STEP 1. Break your story statement or key idea into ideas to study.

Copy your story statement (see Springboard 2, p. 34) or your key idea (see Springboard 1, p. 28) at the top of a sheet of paper. Next, underline all the important words and phrases in your story statement or key idea. List those words, leaving about ten lines between each word. If you are unsure whether or not a word is important, underline it. You can always cross it off the list later.

EXAMPLE (Nonfiction)

>*Key Idea*—Explain the *decline* of *savings* in *America* and how it *affects* the *economy**

decline

savings

America

affects

economy

EXAMPLE (Fiction)

>*Story Statement*—"This is a story about some people who *crash* their *plane* in the *Amazon* and *fight* their way through the *jungle* back to a *small town*."

crash

plane

Amazon

fight

jungle

small town

This is amazingly simple, but it always works. You can use it to break out areas to study for small parts of the project as well as the whole project; for example, write a few sentences describing your main character or write a two-sentence summary of an important scene, then underline the important words and make an areas list. If you are working on an assignment, underline the most important words in the assignment to make the list.

STEP 2. Make a list of pointers

Pointers narrow the area down and point out the types of things within that area you might want to learn. Questions often work best as pointers. If you wish, you can extend this process by writing pointers about pointers.

---

*From *10,000 Ideas for Term Papers, Projects, Reports and Speeches* by Kathryn Lamm (Arco, 1984), a good book for college students who have trouble finding good key ideas. Incidentally, the book includes notes on the difficulty of the library research involved for each idea.

EXAMPLE (Nonfiction)

Areas	*Pointers*
decline	When did the decline begin?
	What was the savings rate before?
	How much have savings declined?
	Was the decline steady?
	How is the decline measured? total dollars?
	percent of gross national product? other?
	Are there other ways to measure it?
savings	How is savings defined? by whom?
	Is the definition accurate or approximate?
	How does the government track savings?
America	How do Americans differ from Japanese, Canadians, English, Germans, Indians, or Argentineans?
	Which of those differences are cultural, which economic?
affects	the average worker
	small business, big business
	government
	employment
	job creation
	trade balance
	inflation or deflation

EXAMPLE (Fiction)

Areas	*Pointers*
crash	What makes planes crash?
	What would the pilot do in a crash?
plane	What kind of plane would be a good one for the story?
	How many passengers do various small planes hold?

Areas	Pointers
Amazon	What part of the Amazon has jungle near it and a good small town to reach?
	What sort of people live there? What language do they speak?
	What's the weather like?
fight	What sort of tools and supplies would be needed to survive, say, ten days in the jungle?
	What kind of food would the passengers be able to hunt or pick? How would they go about it?
jungle	What does it look like?
	What are the names of some of the plants?
	What are the dangers of the jungle?
small town	What does it look like?
	Would it have an airport? boats?
	Would the town people be different from the jungle people?

STEP 3. Begin to list potential sources.

Of course, you may not know many sources until you dig in at the library, but you should start considering the possibilities right away and make a potential source card for any that pop to mind as you read your pointers.

There are four types of sources: library sources, personal interviews, direct observation, and experiments.

a. *Library Sources.* Almost every book, article, or film you need can be found in some library somewhere. You don't need to find all the names of these sources through the subject catalogue. Check the bibliography of every book you read for clues, and ask your professor or the people you interview for suggestions. An abstract is a summary of a book or an article. Many libraries have abstracts on computer data bases: you can usually search through the abstracts for free or for a nominal fee. Don't forget to check the television schedule as well, especially channels with news, documentaries, and public service programs.

Most important, make a potential source card the minute you discover the possible source. (See "Notes from the Pros: On Sources," p. 53, to learn how to write a source card.) Don't tell yourself, "Well, I won't have time to find that anyway." One week later, you may kick yourself for forgetting that name. And never throw source cards away. You may want them for your next project.

b. *Personal Interviews.* Everyone is an "expert" to a writer. It's just a matter of discovering the subject. Hang around writers on their daily rounds, and you'll find them asking the store clerk how the new shoes are working out, debating menu changes with the owner of the local cafe, and sympathizing with the bus driver over schedule changes. Bums will not get a quarter from a writer without first explaining where the best places are to sleep on the street. Writing after doing library research is not the same as writing after discussing the subject with an expert source.

An expert doesn't need a Ph.D. An expert is just a person you could ask questions about the area you are researching. For example, you could talk to a local banker about people's savings habits or to a pilot about planes and airplane crashes. You might know someone who visited the Amazon on vacation or a foreign student from Brazil. Don't forget the college itself. You may find a well-known authority sitting in an office on campus and perfectly willing to give a conscientious student a few minutes.

Interviews can be quick and informal. Look in the events calendar of the campus news or the local paper. You may be able to do informal interviews with hundreds of business leaders, doctors, lawyers, and other groups by dropping in at the lunch hour.

c. *Direct Observation.* You can make yourself into an expert by taking a look on your own and making notes. The rule is: do the obvious, easy observations first. You could go to the Amazon, if you could afford the trip, but you could also watch a television program about the Amazon and take notes. You can look at planes in a local flight museum or a small airport.

d. *Experiments.* If you are going to write a scene where the characters talk while making peanut butter and jelly sandwiches, try making a sandwich for research. Experiments do not need to be complex and scientific. Little, unscientific experiments can help you, too.

STEP 4. Choose Priorities.

Research takes time. You may run out before the deadline, so cover the most important areas first and the least important areas last. First of all cross out any areas or pointers you don't plan to use. Then store one page for each remaining area in a notebook. Write the area at the top of the page and the pointers down below. If one pointer stands out as critical, make a separate sheet for it. Leave space to add more pointers as you read.

Now get tough. Put the sheets in priority order with the most important first and the least important last. When you get to the library, force yourself to tackle them in that order.

Springboard 4: Fact Sheets

Research is to see what everybody else has seen and to think what nobody else has thought.

—Albert Szent-Gyorgyi

If you feel a little nervous about libraries, relax. Many people do. For reasons no one can explain, the first trip to the library on a new research project often causes discomfort, no matter how experienced the researcher. To get past the butterflies, make a fact sheet for each research area on the first day. You will storm the library with ease for the rest of the project. You will also have plenty of specifics right at hand as you burn the midnight oil or run through your manuscript double-checking facts later on.

Try It

Head for the general reference section and find a table where you can spread out. Set out a clean page for each area of your game plan (see Springboard 3, p. 45). Now go on a little treasure hunt through several basic references collecting interesting facts, dates, names, places and, of course, potential sources. Keep going until you have filled an entire page with interesting facts, statistics, names, and dates on each research area.

Four or five general reference books of any kind will do. We suggest the following:

1. *An encyclopedia.* Choose a general encyclopedia, such as the *Encyclopedia Britannica* or an encyclopedia specializing in a field such as physics, history, or architecture. Use the newest version that you can find, and keep in mind that encyclopedias tend to become quickly outdated.

2. *An almanac. The World Almanac and Book of Facts* or *The Information Please Almanac* are available everywhere.

3. *A dictionary.* You can use a general dictionary, such as the *Webster's Third New World Dictionary*, or a dictionary specialized to a particular subject, such as *Barron's Pocket Guide to Literature and Language Terms.*

4. *An Atlas.* Atlases are basically collections of maps, but they may also contain good introductory articles on geography in the front and *gazetteer* in the back listing the populations and locations of towns and cities. For a treat, get the *Times Atlas of World History* which traces human history and population changes.

5. *A statistical reference.* These vary depending on your subject. Check the subject catalogue for statistical references on any particular subject. Try

the *Statistical Abstract of the United States* (Washington Bureau of Census) or *The Statistical History of the United States from Colonial Times to Present.*

6. *An unfamiliar reference.* Choose anything in the reference section that looks interesting. If you try out a new reference each time you research, you will soon be a whiz at finding what you want fast.

    Once you record a fact on your facts sheet, list the name of the source and the page number on which you found it in parentheses. Be sure to make a source card for each reference book you consult. Finally, double check everything to be certain that you have copied numbers, dates, and names correctly. *Note*: If you have trouble finding these basic sources, you need to make friends with a librarian. Hollywood librarians get cross with anyone who tries to use the library; real librarians realize that they work in a treasure house and feel badly that so few people use it. As long as you respect their time and do your own work whenever you can, they are delighted to help you. If the librarian is too busy, ask when business is normally slow and come back. Be sure to show the librarian your game plan and get ideas for sources before you leave.

    One final suggestion: most librarians have pamphlets and/or tours for first time users; ask about them. If you could read all the books in any one library, you would discover that each library has a distinct personality. No two are identical. It only makes sense to introduce yourself.

Springboard 5: Giving Your Characters a Background

The characters have their own lives and their own logic and you have to act accordingly.

—Isaac Bashevis Singer

Whatever happens in your story happens because of characters. Your characters act or react to something. They take those actions because of their backgrounds: their previous experiences, their opinions, and their personalities. Characters are just like real people. They have names, live somewhere, hold jobs, go to school, own pets, and have pet peeves. They get tired and cranky, hold nutty opinions, and have unique goals and frustrations. Part of the fiction writer's background research is getting to know the characters because characters provide the motivation of the story, the reasons for the plot. What your characters learn about themselves and life in general develops the underlying theme of the story. You must know your characters extremely well if you want to make them come alive. It's easy to introduce yourself to your characters. Just ask your characters some questions.

Try It

The character interview filesheet is a list of questions to ask. The questions are written as questions *to* the characters. To use the filesheet, pretend that the character is answering the questions. Try to stand in the character's shoes and look at life through the character's eyes.

INTERVIEW WITH A CHARACTER (FILESHEET)

1. Are you the main character in the story or a secondary character?

2. What is your full name? (*First, Middle,* and *Last*)?

3. Do you have a nickname? What is it? How did you get that nickname?

4. How does your name fit your personality? Do you like your name? Even your middle name?

5. How old are you? What year were you born?

6. Where do you live? Do you live alone or with other people? Who lives with you? Are the people you live with characters in the story?

7. Do you have a job? What is it? Where do you work? What are the hours? How long have you done that job? What did you do before? Do you like your job?

8. Do you go to school? What grade? What's your best subject? What's your worst? Do you like school?

9. How tall are you? What build (thin, medium, heavy, etc.)? How much do you weigh? What color is your hair? Your eyes?

10. Are you rich, poor, or average? Does it matter to you whether or not you have money?

11. Which three of the following traits best describe you:

lazy	clumsy	cheerful	tense	shy
loyal	imaginative	snobbish	good-natured	intelligent
curious	enthusiastic	neat	graceful	unhappy
powerful	careful	thoughtful	lonely	tight-fisted
detached	dull	tough	practical	messy
timid	bold	frustrated	angry	funny
relaxed	critical	sympathetic	outgoing	bubbly
loud	quiet	hard-working	artistic	organized
energetic	intellectual	confused	realistic	a dreamer
fussy	serious			

12. What would you like the most if you could have it?

13. What is your biggest pet peeve?

14. What do other people always tell you about yourself?

15. What is the best thing about you? The worst?

16. When are you the happiest?

17. Choose any three of your answers and write two or three paragraphs explaining those answers.

Notes from the Pros:
On Sources

Sources are research. Research really consists of tracking down your sources, consulting your sources, and cross-checking your sources. Interviews, direct observations, experiments, and surveys are called *primary* sources because the researcher gets the information first-hand. Books, films, and other archival material are called *secondary* sources.

The first rule of sources is: *start with secondary sources.* Your interview with an astronaut, should you be lucky enough to get one, may flop if you don't have solid background in the history of the space program and the astronaut's career. You'll also design better experiments and get more out of direct observations if you've done your homework in the library beforehand.

Tracking down sources is half of research. One source leads to another, so you want to keep careful records of any potential sources you run across as you read books or interview people. Keep an index card for each potential source.

Your list should include a bibliography card for each book, magazine article, film, or data base that you might consult. Office supply stores sell bibliography cards that are well worth the money because the preprinted format ensures that you record *all* the necessary information. Record the following:

Books & Databases	*Articles*	*Films*
author's name(s)	author's name(s)	film company
title and subtitle	magazine name	title & subtitle
publishing date	article title	copyright date
edition number	year, month, & volume	
publisher, city	page numbers	

If you can't find all the information on a potential source just yet, gather as much as you can. A typical source card might look like this:

Panati, Charles. *Extraordinary Origins of Everyday Things.* New York, N.Y.: Harper and Row, 1987.

For collections or reference works, list the editors' names. For data bases, use the book format. (You don't need to list data bases that simply replace the card catalog in the library or help you track sources.)

In addition to source cards for books and films, make a source card for each person you might contact for a personal interview. Include his or her name (double-check the spelling), title(s), place of work, address, telephone number, and a brief listing of his or her major accomplishments.

Make source cards for primary sources as well. Make one card for each personal observation, survey, or experiment. Leave space for recording the dates on which you do the research and space for the names and backgrounds of anyone who helps you do it. Record any other mundane information (the weather? the number of the bus route? the name of the policeman who gave you the ticket for sitting on the grass?) that may get lost if not recorded. If your direct research might produce a lot of raw data, you may also want to note where and how you plan to store the data.

When you consult your source, first update the source card. Double-check the spelling of any names and titles. Triple-check the dates. Fill in any missing information and note the date you consulted the source on the back of the card. This mundane little bit of housekeeping will save you hours of backtracking trying to fill in the data later. Make it a habit.

Talking to someone or reading a book while simultaneously trying to take accurate notes is a little like patting your head and rubbing your stomach at the same time. It takes practice to learn to do it well. Concentrate first on learning to take good notes. Take your time. Hurried notes now mean wasted hours later. Tape recordings can be great back-ups, especially for personal interviews, but do not depend solely on tape recorders for notes. Tapes can break, and more than one writer has discovered how easy it is to record pop tunes on top of precious, one-time-only interviews.

Notes are easier to take with secondary sources. The kind of notes you take depends on both the project and your own preferences. Many people like to use index cards because they are easy to shuffle later on. Try to capture just one thought, quote, or piece of information per card. Take notes in your own words: don't copy. (It is too easy to accidentally plagiarize if you copy your notes verbatim.)

The index card format below works well for most people. The left hand corner contains a word or phrase indicating what the card is about, the right hand corner an abbreviated reference to the source (keep complete source references on your cards.)

EXAMPLE

Neon light, invention of

Neon was discovered in 1898 by William Ramsey and Morris Travers, English chemists. French physicist Georges Claude perfected neon tube in 1909.

Source: *Extraordinary Origins of Everyday Things*, pg.137

Some people *hate* index cards. You should try to learn to take notes on them, but you have other options. Try taking notes in branches (see Springboard 6, p. 57). Write summaries of books or articles. Sprinkle references to the source (including page numbers) through the summary in parentheses.

Reporters notebooks work well, especially if you are on the road and can't carry piles of paper and index cards with you. Just buy a secretarial spiral notepad and take notes strictly in date order as you encounter sources.

Use your imagination to discover your best system for taking notes, but pick your method in advance and stick to it systematically. If you don't like your choice, change all of your notes to a new method—or just wait until the next project to change.

Before you consult a source, give some thought to how you are going to store the materials you gather. The longer the piece, the more vital this is. Just one irritating session scrambling through piles of cryptic, disorganized notes ought to convince you to plan for storage ahead of time. For most projects, a stack of index cards plus a three-ring binder are adequate. Use the cards for source lists and notes, and the binder for copies of the assignment, game plans, outlines, lists and anything else that won't fit on an index card. Large projects may require separate files for storing raw data, interviews, and notes.

Finally, double-check everything. One person's fact is another's fancy. If you ask six eyewitnesses to describe the same incident, you will hear six very different descriptions. Just because something is printed in a book does not mean that it is accurate. Remember the story of the 1631 authorized edition of the *Bible* that said, "Thou shall commit adultery." As Hirsh Goldberg notes in *The Blunder Book*, libraries are really "museums of error." There is no such thing as a perfect book. Try to find two or three sources, especially for important facts on which you plan to rely heavily.

Student's Notebook:
On Vocabulary

As the writer Ugo Betti observed, "Thoughts run on words like beads on a string." Having more words available to you enriches thoughts and gives you the means to express them. You are in luck here. English possesses the richest vocabulary of any language, approximately 600,000 words. A precise, vivid English word exists for almost anything you wish to say.

The average college graduate can recognize about 10,000-15,000 words and can recall about 2,500. Reading draws on your recognition vocabulary, but writing draws on your recall vocabulary. Even those with large recognition vocabularies may want to enlarge their recall vocabulary before they write. Because our recall vocabularies are so small, adding as few as twenty-five or thirty words can be a big help.

Obviously, you can't learn all 600,000 English words by Friday, so your best bet is to work on words related to the piece you plan to write. First, you need to assemble a list of the words related to your subject. One easy way is to draw pictures related to your piece and label them. Make a list of the words on your labels. They will be largely nouns. You may want to check *What's What*, a "pictionary," for more. It has labelled pictures arranged by subject.

As words go, precise nouns and vivid verbs count for more than other kinds of words. To add more verbs to your list just write sentences using your initial list of nouns. Make a list of the verbs. Add any adjectives, and adverbs of interest.

Once you have a pretty good list of words related to your subject already in the recall vocabulary, it's time to expand. Get out a thesaurus or a copy of *Rodale's Synonym Finder*. Look up each word on your list and make a list of synonyms for it. If you are using a thesaurus, list the antonyms as well. The *Synonym Finder* only has synonyms, but you can get antonyms by thinking of one antonym, then looking that up. Remember that synonyms are words with similar meanings, but not the same meaning. The synonyms for blue are azure, turquoise, navy, and so forth—each a slightly different shade of meaning. Check the definitions in a good dictionary of any words on your list whose shades of meaning are not clear to you. Of course, most words have two or more meanings. Blue also means sad. You may want to look up any words whose second meanings you don't remember. Once you have a good long list of words, practice. Write a sentence using each. Try to use some of the words in the course of your daily conversation for the next week. Using words moves them from your recognition to recall vocabulary faster than any other technique.

One last hint: Build your vocabulary as you plan. Give the words time to sink in, time for you to grow comfortable with them. A new word gleaned from a thesaurus as you draft almost always sticks out like a beacon in the night. Once you have absorbed your new vocabulary, the words will come naturally to mind as you draft and fit invisibly into the context of your sentences.

FINDING AN ORDER

You can research the background as much as you want, but the day will come when you must begin to pin down what you want to say and how you want to say it. You have reached the *Order* corner of the writing idea triangle. It is the quirkiest corner of the triangle. No two writers handle it the same way. You must find your own method.

Of course, you will probably first tackle deciding roughly what you want to say, but you won't really be ready to write until you have some idea what you want to say first, what next, and what after that. Writing is sequential; you can only put one sentence on paper at a time. Because thoughts about what to say don't necessarily pop to mind one sentence at a time, the order corner of the triangle includes just about anything you do before you write to collect your scattered thoughts and develop some idea what to cover first, second, and third. In short, any outline.

There are hundreds of ways to outline. P. G. Wodehouse sometimes wrote 120,000 word scenarios for 70,000 word books. Now there's an outline! You probably won't want to get so carried away, so in this last section of the planning chapter, we include two of the most popular simple ways to outline first: branching and designs. If you don't like those, the last Springboard lists another dozen methods.

Choose whatever method helps you, and don't be afraid to write two or three different types of outlines for one piece. The real point of any outline is to build something to support you as you draft. Trying to draft and think simultaneously is hard. The outline lets you do some of the thinking ahead of time and takes some of the pressure off you as you draft.

One final tip: Look on your outline as a flexible guide, not a straitjacket. As you draft, you will outgrow your outline. Don't try to force your piece back into the outline; adjust the outline to keep up with your writing.

Springboard 6: Branching

One of the only virtues of linear outlining is that it looks neat, and that very virtue is its downfall. By working hard to make sure the outline is neat, we effectively cut off any additions and insertions, any new idea.

— Henriette Anne Klauser

Branching is one of the best outlining methods for quickly thinking ideas through and recording thoughts before they disappear. Its other virtue is that it produces a visible picture of a whole piece, so that you can begin to see where your thoughts are heading and chart the relationships between your ideas. You can use branching for more than outlining, incidentally. Branching fans also use it for scheduling, for taking notes, for taking minutes at meetings, for studying, for making grocery lists — you name it. If you want more details on it, see Henriette Anne Klauser's wonderful book *Writing on Both Sides of the Brain* (a must-read for anyone who writes).

Try It

To choose a simple example, let's suppose we are writing an article for a pet magazine or a women's magazine on buying a pet turtle, instead of a cat or a dog.

To make this branch, we started with our writing idea in the center and drew a picture of a turtle just for fun. We could have also used the word turtle instead. The first thing we thought of was the title, "Turtles as Pets." The next idea was to list the advantages of turtles over other kinds of pets. We drew a branch for advantages and listed them on little branches shooting off the main branch. Next we drew a branch for "Food" and collected our ideas about food. The idea of food suggested houses, so we made a branch for "Houses" and collected our ideas about turtle houses. We collected all of our ideas, no matter how trivial or silly they sounded. If we weren't sure about a fact, we just wrote a question mark after it.

Try making a branch outline of your current story or nonfiction piece. There are not really any rules to follow, but here are some things to keep in mind:

- Begin in the center of the paper with a picture or a word representing your writing idea or some part of your writing idea.

- It is perfectly okay to be messy, to draw little pictures, to use colored pens, to use big pieces of paper, or anything else you wish. Don't try to be too pretty about it because that might slow you down. You want to collect your ideas as fast as you can. You can always draw a tidied-up branch later if you wish.

- Remember that ideas come in waves. If you run out of ideas, keep drawing branches and trying to fill them in until the next wave comes. Always try to branch for at least ten minutes, so that you catch more than one wave of ideas.

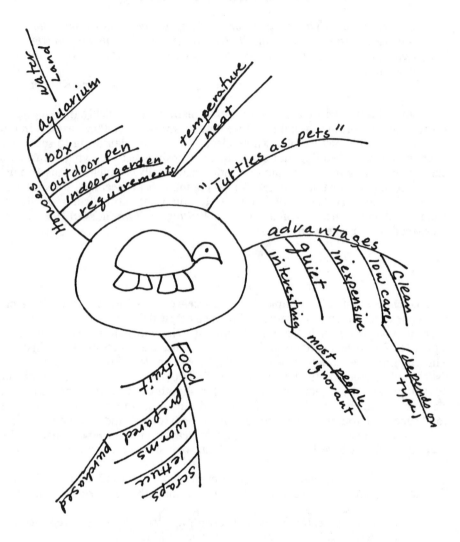

- You don't need to stick to one branch until you finish it. If an idea for another branch comes to mind, go to work on that branch for awhile.

- Record all your ideas, no matter how trivial or silly they seem at first. You can decide which ones to use later.

Springboard 7: The Design

To be simple is the best thing in the world; to be modest is the next best thing. I am not so sure about being quiet.

—G. K. Chesterton

Underlying most good nonfiction is a very simple design. Designs either break a nonfiction piece into manageable sections or suggest an order of presentation. All nonfiction must have a simple plan, a logic behind the writing. This is not a complex outline, just any simple mental picture or pattern that the writer thinks will work. You can actually use your design to help you write your outline. There are a thousand different designs.

Try It

We've collected several possible designs for the filesheet (p. 60). Try one or two designs on your current piece. You may want to follow it up by drawing a branch (see previous Springboard, p. 57) or try one of the outlining alternatives in the next Springboard.

DESIGNS (FILESHEET)

Sequential design. This design is based on steps and the order (or sequence) of those steps. For example, a how-to article explains what to do first, second, and third in the order the reader is supposed to do them.

Past-present-future. This is a popular design where the writer reviews what happened in the past, what's happening now, and what is likely to happen in the future. Examples can be found in most science magazines. Lincoln's Gettysburg Address is another good example.

Most important point to least important point (or least important to most important). This plan is most often used to make a case for a key idea. For example, if you are writing a movie review, your key idea may be that the movie was not worth the price of admission. Using this design, you would either list the most important reasons it was bad first and work back to the least important or the reverse, least important to most important.

Specific to general (or general to specific). This design starts with specific facts or examples and moves to more general statements (or vice versa). For example, if you are explaining how to fly a hot air balloon, you could tell the specific story of how one person does it and then show how this person's method follows general flying rules. You can also go the other way — explain the general rules for flying hot air balloons and give specific examples of one person doing it to illustrate those rules.

Three balanced points. This is the classic design of the traditional essay or paper. The writer chooses three to five points to make about the key idea and expands on each point equally, adding an introduction and a conclusion.

Storyplan. This design is written like a fictional story, but concludes by making a point. For example, you could tell a story about taking a hot air balloon flight, then discuss why people like the sport.

Musical design. This design is often used for speeches. Repetition of phrases or words carry the plan, so the speech sounds almost musical. One of the masters of this design was Martin Luther King, Jr. The best example is his speech, I Have a Dream.

Springboard 8: Outlining Alternatives

He thinks things through very clearly before going off half-cocked.
— General Carl Spatz

Have you ever watched people plan for trips? They are very funny about it. Fenton Quagmire plans his trip by packing everything in the car he might possibly need, including a lot of junk he will never use. He buys maps of everything and tries to plan every step of the trip in little red lines. Betty Blastoff takes off with a dollar in her pocket and a box of cornflakes. She makes up the trip as she goes along.

Planning a piece of writing is just like planning for a trip. The outline is the place you store your maps and anything else you might need along the way. Like Fenton, you can pack every little thing you might need into an outline, or you can blast off like Betty and make it up as you go along. Fenton and Betty are extremes. You may want to plan something in between.

The number of outlining methods is limited only by the imagination. Try some other methods of outlining besides branching and designs. Make two or more outlines when you outline. No one ever said that you are limited to one outline. The point is to come up with something that makes drafting the piece easier. If you want more outlining ideas, Donald Murray has tucked a comprehensive treasury of outlining methods in the middle of his fine book *A Writer Teaches Writing*.

Try It

Try at least two of the outlining methods on the following filesheet.

OUTLINING ALTERNATIVES (FILESHEET)

ARGUMENTS PRO AND CON

On one side of a sheet of paper, write down a point you might make and all the arguments for your point. Flip the page and write a list of arguments against it on the back side. Along this same line, you can use "costs and benefits," "beautiful and ugly," "good luck and bad luck," or any opposing ideas.

A CHRONOLOGY

The chronology is a good organizer. Every nonfiction subject or fictional character or setting has a history of some kind behind it. Few lists are handier than a chronology listing the dates of important events or inventions related to the subject, setting, or characters. Include small bits of information that you find interesting as well. Chronologies take a bit of time to construct, and you need to double-check your dates. Once you start writing, the chronology turns into a gold mine. Nothing is more irritating than wasting a trip to the library to check on a date. The chronology also provides a list of fascinating tidbits for brightening up pieces. Mentioning that the umbrella originated as a status symbol in Mesopotamia around 1400 B.C. might be just the thing to put a little sparkle in a dull paragraph. Chronologies also help fiction writers maintain consistency, so that characters don't accidently graduate from college or have children at age ten. Tolstoy, who accidently made his character Natasha eighteen years old in 1805 but twenty-four in 1809, could have used one when he wrote *War and Peace*.

CHAINING

Write one paragraph of your piece. Choose one sentence from that paragraph. Write it down to start your next paragraph, and write the next paragraph about that sentence. Keep chaining one paragraph to another until you have four or five paragraphs, then cross out the repeat sentences.

EXAMPLE

Peanut butter sandwiches are the most difficult. Spreading the peanut butter tears holes in the bread that are just the right size for the jelly to drip through. Too much peanut butter makes the jelly squirt out the sides with every bite. The gooey results have made peanut butter and jelly the child's favorite sandwich for centuries.

Too much peanut butter makes the jelly squirt out the sides with every bite. Scholars will long debate whether jelly or jam complement peanut butter best. Children favor grape jelly because it squirts nicely and stains permanently.

COLLECTION BOXES

For this method of outlining, divide the piece into several major categories, then collect your facts and ideas under each category. You can start with the subject; for example, divide transportation into air, water, land, and space or divide Benjamin Franklin's life into politics, business, family, hobbies, and inventions. You can also start with your key idea as in the examples below.

EXAMPLE

Key idea: Public art: who decides?

Category 1: Popular public art

Most popular

Least popular

Examples from three cities

Category 2: Types of public art

Sculptures, fountains, murals, practical (e.g., sundials, park benches), signs, gardens, gateways and entrances, building ornamentation, public buildings themselves

Category 3: Selection processes

Competitions give prizewinner the bid

Bids are submitted and selected on a cost basis

Expert committees or citizen committees commission artists

Philanthropic organizations donate the art

Developers, who volunteer or are required to provide funds or sites in large projects, select the pieces

Fiction writers can use categories such as "settings," "characters," "scene ideas," etc. The purpose of making a collection is to store information and ideas where they are easy to find. It is especially useful when you have a lot of background research you will need to review as you write.

CRITICAL PIECES

To make this outline, write certain critical scenes or sections first, then fill the outline in around them using one of the other outlining methods. For example, you could write the conclusion, then use branching, designs, or collection to outline the rest of the piece. Fiction writers can write the scene with the high point or the end, then outline back to the beginning scene.

CUT AND PASTE

Sometimes, it's easiest just to get your ideas written down while they are fresh, then organize them later. In this outlining method, you outline after you write a rough draft. Write a quick rough draft with no concern for the order, just writing whatever comes to mind. Chop the draft up with scissors, and tape it down in a new order. You can use a branch or a design or any other outlining method to decide how to put it back together. Fill in any missing sentences or rewrite sentences that don't fit any more. Voilà! An outline! (Or maybe even a complete first draft.)

LISTS

Any kind of a list can serve as an outline. For example, make a list of the elements you want to cover in the piece. If your piece is about the policy problems posed by the thinning of the ozone layer, you may want to list threats to health, agricultural problems, and legal concerns among the elements you wish to cover. Another use of lists is organizing your research so that you can then make an outline.

ORGANIZATION CHART

This is a good research organizer. Most of the things that you write about include people who are part of some kind of organization: a family, a business, a government department, a team, or a tribe. Draw an organization chart that gives any proper titles and perhaps a description of who each person on the chart is. If you are dealing with individuals, put the proper spelling of the person's name and birth date. Lay the chart out to visually show the relationships between people.

SKETCHING

When artists plan a big painting, they do practice sketches of little parts of the painting first. You can plan your writing with practice sketches as well. Below are a few ideas of the types of things you can sketch:

Fiction

- Describe your main character walking down a hall, getting mad at something, talking with a friend, talking with a stranger, being frightened by something, or feeling enthusiastic about something.

- Describe a character looking at the setting of the story.

Nonfiction

- Pick any idea in your piece and look at it from two points of view. Explain why you agree with the idea, then explain why you disagree with the idea.

- Write a letter to your idea reader explaining why he or she needs to read what you are going to write.

- Write a letter to your writing group explaining how and why you plan to organize your piece a certain way.

- What is the most important idea or piece of information you intend to write about? Why is it more important than some of the other ideas?

- Choose any idea, fact, or instruction in your piece and write an example.

THE SLUGLINE

Newspaper reporters write the stories, but somebody else writes the headlines, so printers use a temporary headline, called a *slug*, to keep track of a story that doesn't yet have a title. A slug describes the story in no more than five words. "Man Bites Dog" is the classic slug. It tells a whole story in just three words. You can plan your pieces or stories with slugs. Write one slug for the overall piece or story, then write slugs for each major section or scene.

EXAMPLE

Overall: Turtles as Pets

Section 1:   Why get a Turtle?

Section 2:   Buying a Turtle

Section 3:   Making the Turtle a Home

Section 4:   Feeding the Turtle

WHAT I KNOW AND DON'T KNOW

This can help you spot holes in your research that may be causing difficulties with your outline. First, list the things you *already* know about the subject (for a nonfiction piece) or the setting or characters (for a fiction piece). Make another list of the things that you *don't* know about the subject. Once you make this list, all of a sudden, you will see twenty more things you don't know. The more you know about a subject, the longer *both* lists, not just the *know* list, are likely to be.

EXAMPLE

Subject: Gothic Cathedrals

What I Know	*Don't Know*
• mid-12th century to end 15th century	• first one?
• developed from Romanesque	• why flying buttresses?
• most popular in France	• what features come from Romanesque
• flying buttresses developed later	• list of Gothic cathedrals, dates
	• why most popular in France? more money? social factors?

Notes from the Pros:
On Fair Play

The old proverb is: teach the writer, not the writing. It is a good rule because writing doesn't always play fair. Despite enthusiasm and immense effort on the part of the writer, some pieces turn to spaghetti and others self-destruct. On the other hand, some seem to write themselves. It's not always clear why one piece won't settle down on the page or collapses altogether, whereas others just flow. With writing, those who sweat most may achieve the poorest results. It isn't fair, but it is part of writing. Most writers have failed manuscripts languishing in the file cabinet.

If you can't seem to make a piece work despite a long struggle, don't punish yourself. You aren't a bad writer. You may learn more from a piece that fails than from a big success. Give yourself credit for trying. Take a breather or move on to something else. Those who persist in the face of such disasters should always get credit for bravery. It's part of learning to fail and try again, and that's a big part of learning to write.

Notes from the Pros:
How Long Will It Take?

You may be interested in knowing how long it takes a professional writer to write something. The man to consult is Lawrence Block. Block, in addition to writing novels, writes a column for *Writer's Digest Magazine* and teaches writing workshops. Block's book, *Writing the Novel: From Plot to Print*, is one of the most practical, honest, and down-to-earth books on actually getting any book — not just a novel — written that we've run across. He became interested in writers' work habits and surveyed them. According to Block, most professionals average four to five pages a day, not counting research and planning or final editing and copyediting. From start to finish, a book a year — including time off between books — is a good output for a professional. That works out to something like one page a day. Then there's Isaac Asimov, who does fifty pages a day, but he is truly unique. You may want to take another look at your planning. How long is this *really* going to take?

Chapter 3

Getting the Words
to Flow on Paper

WRITER'S BLOCK

Every nightmare (and even dogs have them) hints at the secret reserves of imaginative power in the human mind. What the stalled or not-yet-started writer needs is some magic for getting in touch with himself, some key.

— John Gardner

INTRODUCTION

Writing down a telephone message, directions to a friend's house, or the answer to a question on a test is not at all the same as writing a unified story, essay, or report—no more than painting a house is the same as painting a landscape. Drafting a complete piece is a whole new world.

When beginning writers first encounter long, unified pieces, the change is a shock. A person writing down a telephone message knows how long it will take to write it down and has a fair idea what the result will be. Those writing longer pieces soon discover that sometimes they are hot, sometimes stone cold. They cannot estimate whether or not a drafting session will go well, nor can they estimate how long it will take to finish. They are haunted by a sense that the result could easily be an embarrassing catastrophe, understanding what Aldous Huxley meant when he said, "A bad book is as much of a labour to write as a good one; it comes as sincerely from the author's soul." Worse yet, they have trouble deciding how well it turned out once they have finished. This is not a problem for students alone. Working writers often remark that they don't know how a piece turned out, even though they have just reread it. Students may only have a vague sense that they have lost control. Writing suddenly feels like drifting helplessly on the sea in a glass float when it used to feel like rowing a boat. The longer the piece, the more disturbing the sensation.

The rules are upside down in the new world. Puzzling out how to manage takes a long time, especially if no one mentions that it *is* a new world with different rules. Trying to cope under pressure leads a surprising number of people to suffer from writing blocks at an early age. Some find writing so painful that they learn to avoid writing whenever possible.

Avoiding Writing Blocks

The term *writer's block* brings to mind an agonized genius living in a cold sweat, unable to get one line on paper, not a college student, stuck on the third paragraph wishing the assignment would vanish. The fully blocked writer is indeed a rare phenomenon, but almost all those who write face a few garden-variety writing problems at one time or another:

1. They can't get started.

2. They can't find a voice for the piece, and it sounds stilted, phony, or cramped.

3. They write in painful fits and jerks.

4. They can only write occasionally.

5. They can't finish.

6. They suddenly lose confidence in their work.

7. They hit a wall about two-thirds of the way through.

As writer and editor Gene Fowler said, "Writing is easy; all you do is sit staring at a blank sheet of paper until the drops of blood form on your forehead." It is no joke. These obstacles cause more writing failures for students than anything else in writing. If students can't surmount them, all progress ends.

Writing isn't one task, but many different tasks combined. Some tasks require creativity, others objectivity. Unfortunately, it is nearly impossible to be creative and objective at once. This conflict is the basic source of writing blocks.

The Artist and the Craftsman

It is easiest to separate conflicting writing chores and avoid blocks if, instead of telling yourself that you are learning to write, you imagine that you are training two separate people to do different jobs taking turns working on the project. This is not a new idea. One of the first writers to note the split nature of writing was Virgil. There has always been a creative side to writing and an editorial one. Over the centuries, writers have called the two sides of writing many things: "the creator and the critic," "the writer and the editor," "the unconscious and the conscious," "the right brain and the left brain." We call them the artist and the craftsman.*

The Artist's Job Description

The artist is in charge of imagination and drafting. Don't be confused by the term *artist* into thinking we are only discussing fiction. The artist also drafts

---

* Female craftsmen tell us that they still prefer craftsman to craftswoman or craftsperson because the substitutes sound so clumsy—the very thing good craftsmen aren't. We bow to their choice.

snappy business letters, clear lab reports, thoughtful commentaries, and winning legal briefs as well as riveting dialogue and vivid description because the artist supplies the basic materials of any written piece:

word flow	sentences	paragraphs
ideas	individuality	natural voice
rhythm	style	images
metaphors	analogies	observation
mood	whimsy	unity of thought
organizational unity	patterns	synthesis

The Craftsman's Job Description

The craftsman is in charge of organization and editing, a sort of business manager for the artist. The craftsman:

- decides when, where, and how long the artist will write

- puts together plans and outlines

- analyzes and judges the drafts

- gives the artist suggestions for revision

- finds the proper detail or word when the artist's choice isn't quite right

- polishes and produces the final piece

- deals with teachers, editors, and readers

Happily, there are just two ground rules for writing free of blocks:

1. *Separate the artist from the craftsman.*

    Each has a different job. If you try to do them simultaneously, you can do neither one well. Never mix drafting—the artist's job—with planning or editing—the craftsman's job. Drafting needs word flow and enthusiasm. Editing, on the other hand, requires judgment and detachment. Judging interferes with word flow, and detachment dampens enthusiasm. You cannot possibly do them simultaneously.

    Spelling, punctuation, vocabulary, and presentation also belong to the craftsman and should never be considered during early drafts.

Concern over them will slow down the drafting and break the artist's train of thought. On the other hand, setting up the work conditions is the craftsman's job. When the artist does it, it's called daydreaming, not writing.

There are a number of ways to separate the work of the artist and the craftsman. The easiest is simply to leave time between doing the chores of the artist and those of the craftsman. For example, don't try to draft and edit in the same session. Don't even try to plan and draft in the same session. Try to leave at least twenty-four hours between tasks.

You may also want to give your personal artist and craftsman names to separate the two more clearly. Anything that helps you mentally divide the two is worth trying.

2. *Give the artist and the craftsman equal standing and train them to equal strength.*

One is not "better" than the other. A weakness in one weakens both. If the craftsman becomes too strong, too critical, or interferes too soon, the artist is blocked. The words don't flow and there isn't much for the craftsman to prune and shape later. On the other hand, the artist is a bit lazy. Without the help of the craftsman, the piece may never be finished. Both the artist and the craftsman must be equally strong, working in harmony.

There is a little artist in each of us. To tap into your creative powers, you only need to know one thing: *the artist is already there.* One of our students called his artist "The Force," the invisible power of the Jedi knights in the *Star Wars* movies. Luke Skywalker finds his artist by simply learning to use The Force. He doesn't need to create The Force; he just needs to learn how to release it and then how to direct it. That is exactly how writers train their artists.

This chapter belongs to the artist in you. The first group of springboards in this chapter — "Early Morning Freewrite," "Creative Concentration," and "Braindancing and Downhilling" — helps you release the artist within. The remaining activities help you begin to control and direct your artist. Be prepared to have fun, and try to make the business of drafting as magical as you can. The artist thrives on magic.

Springboard 1: Early Morning Freewrite

... If you are to have the full benefit of the richness of the unconscious, you must learn to write easily and smoothly when the unconscious is in the ascendent.
— Dorothea Brande

In her wonderful book *Becoming a Writer*, Dorothea Brande points out that the easiest way to release the artist is to write first thing in the morning. Although it is difficult to dig yourself out of bed to do this regularly, early morning freewriting does noticeably improve the work of those who do it regularly.

Try It

Put your personal journal and a good free-flowing pen on the nightstand before you go to bed. Get up a few minutes earlier than usual, sit up in bed, and start writing before doing *anything* else—including brushing your teeth. Write about anything that happens to come to mind for a few minutes. Let yourself drift from thought to image. Avoid directing your writing. If you can't think of anything to say, write about your empty mind. You'll soon drift to some subject. Don't look at your writing. Just put it away.

After you have done this every day for a couple of weeks, take a look at your journal. You'll find a lot of junk, but also some writing that is so terrific you won't believe you wrote it. We don't know why this happens. Somehow early in the morning your artist is awake even though, or perhaps because, the rest of you is half asleep.

Many people who like this activity don't use the freewrites for writing projects. They want to be truly free to record whatever trivia or trash comes to mind in the morning, unconfined by a plan or a deadline. According to the freewriting fans, even if the early morning freewrite is inconsequential, all other writing that day seems easier and turns out better. It's as if the morning freewrite taps some inner channel to your artist that stays open for the rest of the day.

Springboard 2: Creative Concentration

What a release to write so that one forgets oneself, forgets one's companion, forgets where one is or what one is going to do next—to be drenched in sleep or in the sea. Pencils and pads and curling blue sheets alive with letters heap up on the desk.

—Anne Morrow Lindbergh

Many people say that writing takes discipline. This is only partly true. What writing absolutely requires is focused concentration. Achieving that concentration requires discipline. The reason concentration is so important is that the artist comes out when you concentrate. Unfortunately, concentration is hard to force. "Concentrate!" you tell yourself clenching your fists. Sometimes it works. Often, it doesn't.

There is another way to concentrate. We call it creative concentration. Think back to doing something you really enjoyed. Did you ever become so involved that you didn't notice the time or what was happening around you? That's creative concentration. It's a little like daydreaming, except you aren't just dreaming. You are *doing*. Creative concentration is the best kind of concentration for writing.

Because a writer won can't concentrate is in hopeless shape, treat this activity as a ritual. It will help you build and focus your concentration before drafting sessions. You may want to use it several times during a long writing session or any time you feel tired, distracted, or frustrated.

Try It

The steps to creative concentration are quite simple, but they are almost the opposite of clenching your fists and trying to force it.

1. Relax and clear your mind of other things.

2. Focus on what you want to write about.

3. Once your concentration is focused, start writing and keep going without stopping for a little while until you've gotten rolling.

STEP 1. Relax and clear your mind of other things.

For most people, the best time to write is usually early in the morning because they are relaxed and don't have other things on their minds yet. At other times it helps to know how to deliberately relax and clear your mind. Almost any standard relaxation exercise such as the one below will do.

- First, relax your muscles. You can't clear your mind if the rest of you is tense. Take a good stretch. Stretch like a cat. Stretch all your muscles. Lift your shoulders up to touch the bottom of your ears, then let them drop. Stretch your arms up as far as you can. Still stretched, move them around in a big circle. Clasp your hands behind your back and then bend over, stretching your arms up.

- Sit down and close your eyes. Starting with your feet, tense your muscles as tight as you can. Tense them a little more, then suddenly relax. Next, tense your leg muscles and relax. Keep tensing and relaxing muscle groups until you reach the top of your head.

- Next, take deep breaths. With your arms and legs uncrossed and your eyes closed, take a deep breath. Hold it a second, then slowly breathe out. Take another. Slowly breathe out. A few deep breaths put oxygen into your system—nature's way of relaxing people.

- Clear your mind of other thoughts. Sit very still with your eyes closed and picture a wall painted all one color. You can also picture an ocean beach, a pretty meadow, or the soft morning light in an old house. If some thought drifts into your mind, gently push it aside and picture the colored wall or the scene again. Keep returning to the color of the wall or the details in the scene, and you will soon be able to think without distracting thoughts intruding. You want your mind to be as still and peaceful as your body. When your mind is quiet, move the the next step.

STEP 2. Focus on what you want to write about.

Think about the characters, an interesting fact, the first sentence, or anything else about the piece you want to write. Just let the thoughts about it float into your head. Don't try to analyze them. After a couple of minutes, think about what you might write down first. Don't start writing yet. Let your thoughts expand and build for a few minutes.

STEP 3. Start writing and keep going without stopping.

Start writing and write for at least three to five minutes wihtout stopping. You don't need to write fast, just don't go back to make changes or corrections. The point is to start gently and then keep writing without stopping. It won't take long before you are rolling. It is a little like starting a car by rolling it down a hill. That first five minutes is your first push to get your writing car rolling. If you can't think what to say, write "I can't think what to say" or nonsense words. Let the movement of the pen lead you into writing. If you like braindancing (see next springboard), braindance for at least five minutes without stopping, then downhill for another five.

Springboard 3: Braindancing and Downhilling

True ease in writing comes from art, not chance
As those move easiest who have learned to dance.
—Alexander Pope

Writing is not putting words on paper; it's putting thoughts on paper. Many writers say that the best way to achieve style is to avoid thinking about words as you draft. Concentrate instead on telling your reader your thoughts as honestly and precisely as possible. Style follows naturally from honest communication.

This is good advice, but it poses a problem: it takes practice to hold a piece of writing in your mind until you put it on paper. Most of us have trouble writing down our thoughts, largely because thoughts flow so quickly and writing them down takes so long. By the time we record one idea, we have forgotten the next three. In our rush to write down our thoughts before they vanish, we tend to write too quickly, jumping like rabbits from point to point, never developing a complete thought. The result seems thin and disorganized when we read it later.

This activity teaches you a method of exploring and rapidly recording your thoughts before you begin to write. Once you gather your thoughts, then you can slow down, writing about one idea at a time.

We used to call this method brainstorming and fast-writing, but our students would choose Wagnerian-sized themes and write like a sprinter heading for the tape. The process is much lazier; let ideas dance to mind, record them quickly, and then slip gracefully down the page like an expert downhill skier on the last run of the day—braindancing and downhilling.

This and similar methods have been popular for a number of years and go by many different names. Gabrielle Rico calls it clustering or webbing in her book, *Writing the Natural Way*, Henriette Anne Klauser uses branching (see chapter 2) together with rapidwriting to achieve the same results in her book *Writing on Both Sides of the Brain*, and Tony Buzan uses mind-mapping as a follow-up to reading and prelude to writing in *Use Both Sides of Your Brain*. The important point with all of these techniques is to gather your thoughts first, to slow down as you draft, and to avoid attempts at perfection on the first draft.

Try It

Before you start, take a tip from us: get organized first. You don't want to break your concentration by hunting around for pens and paper or thumbing through research notes. Review your notes and organize everything you will need, so that you can find it later without long pauses.

Incidentally, try using different colored pens and pencils to braindance. Some people have an incredible urge to make their writing look pretty; in a first draft they should not. Using pretty colors to braindance satisfies this urge and reduces the pressure to draft beautifully (and perfectly) the first time.

How to Braindance

The process of braindancing involves the following steps:

STEP 1. Choose a writing idea.

Braindancing and downhilling seem to work best on a small scale. You can use the writing idea for a complete poem or a very short piece. If you are working on a longer story or paper, choose an idea covering just one scene or section of the work. You can chain together your results to make up the complete draft. If you can't think of an idea, use *breakfast* the first time. Almost everyone can think of something to say about breakfast.

STEP 2. Record your writing idea.

On a clean sheet of paper write a word or a phrase in capital letters in the middle of the page. Draw a circle around it. This word or phrase represents your writing idea (or at least a starting point). If you are working on a section of a longer piece, it represents your idea for that section.

STEP 3. Develop creative concentration (see Springboard 2).

STEP 4. Record your thoughts as they come to you.

To record a thought, just write down a couple of words that will help you remember the thought later on. For example, suppose you are writing a nostalgic story about a pet dog you owned as a child, and one of your thoughts is, "the dog chewed pink tennis shoes." You could record it by writing (dog) or (dog shoes) or (pink shoes) . Later, as you draft the story, simply looking at these words would remind you of the thought.

Put a circle around each thought after you record it. The circle is important. It separates one thought from another and makes each thought easier to remember. Draw lines between thoughts that you think are connected so that the page ends up looking like a spiderweb of thoughts.

Don't try hard and don't hurry. Also, don't try to decide if the thoughts are good or not. Don't even try to decide if you will use a thought in the draft or not. Just let the thoughts come and record them—whatever they are. Remember the principle of creativity: get the ideas down first, make judgments later.

EXAMPLE

Writing Idea: A story about a stubborn dog named Harry.

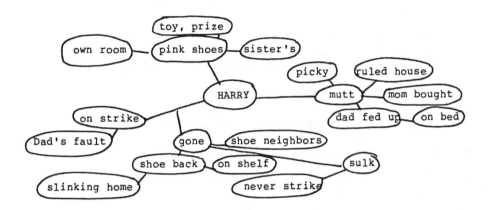

Below are some of the thoughts written out in sentences:

"Harry was a mutt that Mom brought home one day. Harry soon tried to rule the whole house. He was picky, too. He insisted on having his own room. He took a pink tennis shoe from my sister's closet and wouldn't give it back. It was his toy, his prize. Finally, when Harry decided to sleep on Dad's bed, Dad got fed up and tried to boot him off. The next morning Harry was gone. And so was his shoe...."

How to Downhill

Pick one thought on your braindance as a place to start and start writing. Take it easy. Don't hurry. Remember, you are an expert skier gliding gently down the slope. Keep writing until you get to the end of your piece. If you are writing a long piece, write a section or a scene in one downhill glide. You can pause to look at your braindance (or to add to it), but don't stop for too long.

It's vital to keep moving down the page. Don't erase, cross out, or back up. Fiddling with details and backing is like skiing uphill. Besides wasting energy, it doesn't work. Fix details and problems later. You want to feel free and easy when you downhill.

Incidentally, be sure to leave big margins and write on one side of the page using every other line. If you decide to edit later on, it will be a lot more work if you don't leave space for it now. You also won't be able to cut and paste if you've written on both sides of the page.

Further Tips on Braindancing and Downhilling

- If you think of something for another part of the piece, don't wait. You'll forget it. Record it on your braindance or add it in the margins drawing an arrow to the place it should go. You can also write your additions on a separate sheet of paper. Label them with different numbers, such as "ADD #1" or "ADD #2". Note where it should go by writing "ADD #1" at the place where you want to insert it.

- When you are drafting, you may sometimes bump into something Henriette Anne Klauser calls *THE WALL*. This is just the place where you are having trouble keeping going. Writers know it very well. Here's the trick: never stop writing at the wall. Plod along one sentence at a time for awhile. Tell yourself that you will keep writing for five more minutes. The wall doesn't go on forever. If you keep plodding, you will suddenly go right over the wall and breeze on through to the end.

- Go back and add to your braindance until you feel like writing again.

- If you must stop because you've run out of time, pick up the next time by braindancing some more. You might also try recopying the last paragraph and then continuing your downhill. Some writers like to edit their previous drafts as a way to get back into writing. You can try this, but most beginners find it easier to save editing until they have everything down on paper.

- If you constantly slow down because you can't remember a word, a spelling, or a punctuation rule, don't skip over it. Make your best guess, mark it with an "unsure code," and then move on. Unsure codes help you find problems again, so you can fix them when you edit. They do something else, too. Looking up the spelling or punctuation will break your writing concentration. On the other hand, skipping it entirely may leave you vaguely anxious. That breaks your concentration as well. The unsure codes let you do something about the problem without shattering your focus on writing. They are indispensible for those who get butterflies just thinking about grammar, punctuation, and spelling. The middle of a draft is no time to beef up on the use of semi-colons.

  Print the unsure codes in capital letters and put parentheses around them, so that they will be easy to see when you edit. You can make up your own codes. Here are the ones we like to use:

  (SP) = check spelling.

  (PUNCT) = check punctuation.

  (WORD) = find a better word.

  (FACT) = double check this fact.

  (CHECK _____ .) = check whatever
  is noted in the blank space.

Springboard 4: Between Friends

As a rule, what is out of sight disturbs men's minds more seriously than what they see.

— Julius Caesar

Anxiety about the topic, the genre, or some other feature of the writing is perhaps the chief obstacle to writing. It produces an inability to start or finish. This odd little exercise in which the writer has a heart-to-heart chat with the source of the anxiety is useful as a jump-start for those who are anxious about a writing assignment.

Try It

To do this, first pick a writing idea, a starting point, or anything else about the writing that you want to think about. Then make your writing idea or starting point into an imaginary person to whom you can talk. Ask your starting point a question from the filesheet below, then pretend that you are the starting point and write down an answer. Keep asking questions and answering them. Yes, this exercise is a little odd. But it works. That's what counts.

BETWEEN FRIENDS (FILESHEET)

Questions to make your starting point (or writing idea) into someone or something to whom you can talk:

1. What do you look like? A person? Something else? How tall are you? Skinny or fat? How are you dressed?

2. Where do you come from? When did you start? When did I first meet you?

3. Do I like you? Why do I like you? Why don't I like you?

4. Do you help people? What ways do you help people?

5. Are you ever mean to people? How are you mean to people?

6. What is the most interesting thing about you? the least interesting? What is the strangest thing about you?

Questions to help you get to know the starting point or writing idea better:

7. What do I know about you?

8. What don't I know about you?

9. What have I read about you? seen in movies or on television?

10. Who is most interested in you? Why are they interested?

11. What is the one word that best describes you?

12. What is the best thing that ever happened because of you? the worst?

13. Have you changed recently? How?

14. What would I most like to know about you?

Questions to help you understand your feelings about the starting point:

15. What can writing about you do for me?

16. If you were a good friend and could tell me one thing about yourself, what would that be?

17. What is the biggest problem I have with writing about you?

18. What could I do to make writing about you easier?

19. What would help me get started writing about you?

20. How will talking with you like this help me write about you?

21. Is there anything else that I should know about you?

22. (Make up your own question to ask the starting point or writing idea.)

Springboard 5: Finding a Writing Place

The place isn't important. The color of ink or typewriter ribbon isn't important. The fancy files behind your desk or table aren't important. Not being distracted from turning out a page or more a day is important.

—Robert Aldeman

The previous springboards dealt with the psychology of writing, but you should not ignore the physical side of writing. Your surroundings affect your results. We're not saying that writing in a gloomy room produces gloomy work. It's more subtle than that. Some environments aid concentration while others don't, and each person reacts differently to different surroundings. You may prefer writing in a dark corner of the library or you may prefer a sunny windowsill. You may hate fluorescent lighting or love it. The point is to be aware of your physical surroundings and write in places that work best for you. Most writers try to work in the same place at the same time every day or every other day. This habit conditions their minds to focus automatically on writing in that place.

Try It

Find a good writing place and establish the habit of writing in that place long before you face a deadline. Tonight, make a list of possible places. Choose the one that seems closest to your requirements and go there every day for the next week to write. If you don't have an ongoing writing project, work in your practice journal. If, after a week, you are satisfied, keep using it. If not, choose another place from the list and give it a week's trial.

There is no particular place that works for everybody, but there are a few basic rules:

RULE 1. No distractions.

Find a place which doesn't have too many things around to distract you. Talking and writing don't mix. If the words come out of your mouth, they won't flow from your pen. Avoid places where other people interrupt you, talk near you, or where you are tempted to talk yourself. Even pieces of paper or books on your desk can be distracting, so avoid messy places, cramped places, or places where you can't move distracting things out of your field of vision.

Some people find *too much* quiet distracting. They like a little background noise. The trick is to make that noise boring. Foot-tapping music and interesting television programs are no good. Very soft, slow music might be fine. You can buy tapes and records of the sounds of nature: birds, waterfalls, raindrops, etc. These work very well as nondistracting background noise.

RULE 2. Same time, same place.

Always go to your writing place when you want to write. Like jogging, it's better to do a little every day than a marathon session once a week. Writing is exhausting work. Most people cannot handle much more than four hours at a time. In addition, try to find a place you can use at the same time every day. Just the habit of writing at 4:00 P.M. will improve your concentration. Finally, avoid doing other things there. It's your writing place. Save it for writing.

RULE 3. Keep your materials together.

It's best to store your materials at the writing place. If you cannot store them on site, make a tote bag just for writing. Include your writing ideas notebook, practice journal, pens, pencils, paper, yesterday's drafts, notes, and anything else you might need. Don't include things not related to writing. Sometimes, even an accounting text can seem more fascinating than wrestling with a tricky paragraph.

RULE 4. Notice what helps and what doesn't.

As you use your writing place, notice the things that help you and the things that distract you. Experiment with small changes. Keep notes on ideas you have to make your writing place better, but implement the changes slowly. Keep those that help and jettison those that don't seem to help.

Of course, once you have established the writing habit, you may want to vary your pattern just for fun. If you are going to break out of your rut, do it in a big way. Move to the airport, a park bench, or the back row of municiple court. Get up at 4 A.M. for a three-hour session. You may discover something to add to your usual routine, and, who knows, the new scenery may inspire something fabulous.

Notes from the Pros: On Talking About It

Many books on writing suggest (as we do) that students talk about what they are going to write, but the professionals tend to share Norman Mailer's view: "It's hard to talk about one's present work, for it spoils something at the root of the creative act. It discharges tension."

You may also feel that talking about your work makes drafting more difficult, even though others find talking helpful. The middle course may be best. Discuss the possibilities for a piece as you plan, but once you begin drafting, don't talk about it until you have the whole draft on paper. If you encounter a problem during drafting, try to solve it on your own. If you need more help, discuss solutions to that particular problem with a teacher or friend. Once you have an idea how to solve the problem, don't talk it through. Run back to your desk and put your solution on paper before the inspiration cools.

Student's Notebook:
On Coaching

For many people learning to pour words onto paper may seem about as natural as learning to swing a golf club. It feels about the same as holding a long club in a miserably uncomfortable grip and trying to swing smoothly as you bend your knees, keep your head still, shift your weight, not raise your hip, keep your left arm straight, and remember which direction you are hitting the ball. "Relax!" says the coach. It's a wonder more golf coaches aren't clubbed to death. Writing students have similar thoughts about their teachers.

Getting words to flow on paper without too much self-editing is the writer's equivalent of learning to hit the golf ball at the driving range with an easy swing. Coaching does help, but until you develop confidence in your word flow (and relax), all the instructions and rules shouted from the sidelines can be disconcerting. If at any time you become flustered by comments from teachers, friends, or fellow writers, stop listening. Take a deep breath and go back to your practice journal alone. Do the activities that help you concentrate and just try to put some words—any words—on paper. Don't show them to anybody. This is your driving range, and you are only learning to hit the ball, not trying to play like Arnold Palmer. Once you have your word flow going again, you can listen to others' comments. But try to take them one at a time.

DIRECTING THE ARTIST

The remaining springboards in this chapter provide a gentle introduction to controlling your writing. The first, "Zoom Lens," teaches you a simple method for adding sparkle to your writing through the use of detail. The second, "Hooks and Leaders," gives you ideas for writing those all-important first sentences. Next, "Warm-ups for *Cold* Days," has tips for making yourself write even when you are writing cold and don't want to do it. Finally, "Follow the Leader" shows you a general purpose method for learning just about anything you want to learn about writing. The next chapter covers writing techniques to give you even more control.

Springboard 6: Zoom Lens

Every child is an artist. The problem is how to remain an artist once he grows up.

—Pablo Picasso

Nature designed children to write delightful poetry and fiction. Their nonfiction can be very funny, largely because of its inaccuracies. But even in nonfiction, it is their keen observation of detail—details adults have long ceased to notice—that makes their writing sing with originality. The heart of writing is in the detail. The perfect metaphor or description makes the difference between a flat cliché and delight; the great example, between solid nonfiction and a vague opinion. Those metaphors, descriptions, and examples come from observing details. This activity helps you see those details, to once again view the world through the sharp eyes of a child.

Try It

"Zoom Lens" comes from a favorite rule of writers: *Show, Don't Tell.* For example, suppose you are describing a character named Mr. Brown. You could write "Mr. Brown was nice." This is not very interesting. It doesn't show us anything about Mr. Brown. "Mr. Brown was wonderfully nice" or "Mr. Brown was charming" aren't much better. You want to *show* your reader what your characters are like, don't *tell* your reader about them. In other words, show Mr. Brown doing nice things, don't just say he was nice.

EXAMPLE (describing a character)

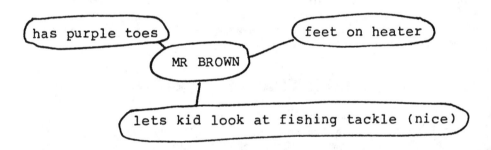

Mr. Brown had purple toes. He ran a small hardware store in town, the kind of store that had one of just about everything. Sunday afternoons, when business was slow, he'd sit up front and let me wander through the store. My favorite section was the fishing tackle. I'd gloat over every new spinner and weight, dreaming that some day I could actually buy one. He'd take off his shoes and socks and put his feet right on top of the small electric heater he kept by the cash register. I asked him once why his feet didn't burn.

"See them toes?" he asked. "They're purple, cold as ice all winter. Can't get 'em warmed up enough to burn."

See how much more interesting Mr. Brown is when the writer shows Mr. Brown being nice? In the course of describing Mr. Brown, the example told quite a lot of the story, too. The reader knows the story takes place in a small town and also meets the character of the child who likes to look at fishing tackle in Mr. Brown's store.

How to Play Zoom Lens

STEP 1. Create a picture of a character in your mind. Put your character in a place—the setting.

STEP 2. Pretend to be a camera operator filming the scene. Look at your scene through the camera.

STEP 3. Once you have the scene set in your mind, zoom in on at least three details about what your character looks like, what your character does, or how your character feels.

STEP 4. Use the details from step three to write a paragraph or two describing the character and/or the setting.

Now try Zoom Lens in your practice journal. Start with a simple sentence describing the character such as "Mr. Brown was nice." Use Zoom Lens to create interesting details, then expand the sentence into a paragraph using those details.

Zoom Lens also helps you describe settings. Normally, you don't describe the setting all at once. You describe it a little at a time as the action of the story takes place. Suppose you want to describe some of the setting by describing a character looking at the sunset. You could write "the sky was beautiful" or you could use Zoom Lens to show your reader details.

EXAMPLE (describing a setting)

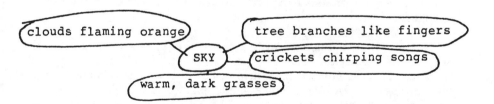

    Joe stared at the setting sun watching the clouds flame orange and melt soft pink. The trees stood in a row along the crest of the hill, black-fingered branches dancing to the songs of crickets in the warm, dark grass. Joe sighed. She hadn't noticed him. So what? Girls never noticed him. It's so shallow to feel bad about it, he thought.

See how much better a reader can picture the sunset? how much better the details of the flaming clouds and singing crickets contrast with Joe's thoughts? Now try describing a setting in your practice journal.

If you have trouble fixing a scene in your mind, try making up at least three details for each of the five senses. Start with something simple, such as "girl sitting on a rock." Pretend you're the girl. Make up at least three details describing how it smells, tastes, feels, sounds, and looks to be sitting on that rock. Top it off by imagining your character's feelings at that moment. You probably won't use all the details you create, but you'll have plenty of ideas.

EXAMPLE (using the five senses)

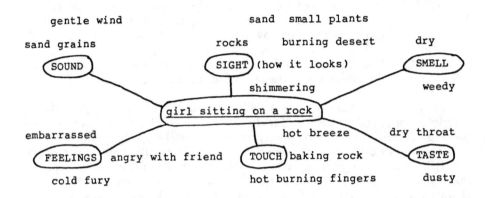

Mary crouched down and tested the warmth of the rock with her fingertips before settling on it. She stared across miles of shimmering rock and sand. Usually the dusty smell and the gentle press of the hot breeze calmed her. But not today. Today, the warm desert brought cold fury.

Try using the five senses to write a description of either a character or a setting in your practice journal.

You can also use Zoom Lens to help you describe a character's mood, such as *bored, happy,* or *frightened.* For example, picture yourself in a place that is boring. Use Zoom Lens to pick out at least three details of the scene. Use the five senses to get more details, if you wish. Then write a couple of paragraphs of a story about a character being bored *without using the words bored or boring.*

The list of words below are good clues that it's time to try a little Zoom Lens. They tend to pop up next to *was* (or *is*) when you are telling, not showing.

TELL WORDS

About Characters	About Settings
was nice	was beautiful
was pretty (or beautiful)	was warm
was ugly	was cold
was friendly	was dark
was sad	was sunny
was bored	was scary
was interesting	was strange
was dumb	was spooky
was lazy	was boring
was funny	was empty
was terrific	was dirty
was smart	was wet
was a pain in the neck	
was tall, dark, and handsome	

One final note. Keen descriptive detail is as vital to nonfiction as to fiction. We used fictional examples in this activity, however, because it is much easier to learn to select the telling detail and to weave it into the story with fiction. Once you have built up the skill through writing a fictional practice piece, you will be able to weave descriptive detail into your nonfiction with ease.

Springboard 7: Hooks and Leaders

Beginning a book is unpleasant ... Worse than not knowing your subject is not knowing how to treat it, because that's finally everything. —Phillip Roth

If you always struggle with your opening, join the club. The first few sentences of any piece are always hard work. On the other hand, the lead is important, so you want those first sentences to be especially good. This activity shows you ten good models you can use. There are thousands of ways to write a lead, so don't limit yourself to these ten. Consider them the start of your collection. As you read, collect good openings. Study them. Try your own versions. Practice writing openings independent of writing complete pieces. Learning to write good leads requires more practice than one lead per story will ever provide.

Try It

You want your opening to grab your reader's attention and then make your reader want to keep reading. It helps to think of a lead as two sentences: *the hook* to grab your reader's attention and *the leader* to carry him into the piece. Just like a fishing line: the hook grabs the fish; the leader drags it into the boat. What hooks a reader? Information, surprises or suspense. What leads the reader on? Knowing a little bit more about what is to come, but not everything. In fiction, the leader sets up a little puzzle to be solved by reading on. In nonfiction, the leader promises more information for the reader who keeps reading.

The "Hooks and Leaders Filesheet" (p. 89) lists ten different kinds of hooks to give you some ideas. Let's look at one of them as an example—the *shocker*. We need a fiction and a nonfiction writing idea to start. Suppose you want to write a fantasy story about a girl and a dragon. We'll name the girl Jesse. Fantasies often have magicians, many of them named Merlin. We like magicians, so we'll make one up. Marlon the Magician. For nonfiction, let's use an article on the benefits of seatbelts. (We are quite sure you can come up with more creative ideas, but these will do for now.)

The shocker hook is based on surprising the reader with a life or death—or at least dangerous—situation. Then we'll add a leader that creates a little suspense. (The hook is in italics. The rest is the leader.)

EXAMPLE (a shocker hook)

> *A purple dragon can change you life or squash you flat.* When Marlon sent the dragon to Jesse, he couldn't be sure which would happen. He just hoped for the best.

Not bad. The shocker presents a scary choice: change or be squashed. The leader gives the reader a puzzle. We learned that Marlon sent the dragon, but we don't know everything. If dragons are so dangerous, why did he send it? Does he hate Jesse? No. The next sentence says he hoped for the best. He's worried. He obviously was forced to send the dragon, but we don't know why or what will happen without reading on.

EXAMPLE (a nonfiction shocker)

> *If you don't buckle up this morning, you could be dead by noon.* If people knew the facts, they would buckle up more often.

In our nonfiction sample, the shocker hook grabs the reader's attention, while the leader promises facts.

Choose a writing idea and try writing at least three different hooks and leaders for the story using the examples on the Hooks and Leaders filesheet as models. This next week, collect the openings of everything you read. Underline the hook and give it a name. Add the best of these hooks to the collection on the filesheet.

Before you begin, notice the hooks and leaders examples based on a children's fantasy. It would not take much revision to make these into the leads for an adult fantasy, would it? The intelligent child is one of the best ideal readers for hooks and leaders because children demand that writers be crystal clear and get to the point fast. As a rule, you also want your lead to get the story or article off to a quick, clean start no matter who is reading it. So try thinking of a sharp eleven-year-old reader as you write hooks and leaders. You can revise them later for your intended audience. It won't take much revising. Adults prefer writers who are clear and get off fast as well. If your style tends to be wordy or stiff, you might want to try writing a whole first draft for a sharp eleven-year-old. It will both loosen you up and also force you to be concise and clear. Good practice.

HOOKS AND LEADERS (FILESHEET)

1. SHOCKER: The shocker hook opens the story with a life or death (or at least dangerous) situation.

   Fiction example: *A purple dragon can change your life or squash you flat.* When Marlon sent the dragon to Jesse, he couldn't be sure which would happen. He just hoped for the best.

   Nonfiction example: *If you don't buckle up this morning, you could be dead by noon.* Too many people take this risk every day.

2. SUMMARY: The summary hook tells the reader who, what, when, where, why, and how in one compact sentence.

   (who)   (what)   (how)   (where)
   Fiction example: *When Jesse saw the purple dragon appear in the meadow*

   (when)   (why)

   one Friday, she knew Marlon the Magician had sent it. Marlon always sent something on Friday, and it usually caused trouble.

   (who) (how)   (what)   (why)
   Nonfiction example: *Each time you buckle your seatbelt, you reduce your chances of being injured or killed that day by fifty percent.* Seatbelts may have saved more lives in the past twenty years than any other human invention.

3. CAPSULE: The capsule hook jumps right in with a brief wrap up or a shorter summary than the full summary hook.

   Fiction example: *Marlon the Magician usually sent something on Friday, and it usually caused trouble, and the purple dragon was no exception.* Jesse, of course, didn't know it, but this particular purple dragon was sent to save her life.

   Nonfiction example: *Seatbelts may have saved more lives in the past twenty years than any other human invention.* Even more lives can be saved if each of us takes a few seconds to buckle up each time we get in a car.

4. DEFINITION: The definition hook begins with either a real definition from the dictionary, or—more fun—one you make up.

   Fiction example: *Dragons are huge, terrifying beasts with beautiful, jewelled eyes and disgusting breath. The friendly ones are purple.* It was the purple variety that met Jesse in a meadow one Friday.

   Nonfiction example: *A seatbelt is something you spend three seconds buckling to save three years in the hospital.* The simple act of buckling up each time you get in a car reduces your chance of getting injured or killed by fifty percent.

5. PROBLEM: The problem hook briefly suggests a problem that you are going to solve in the piece.

    Fiction example: *If a large purple dragon drops into a meadow in front of you one day, it won't go away until you understand why it came.* Jesse knew Marlon had sent the dragon, but she hadn't the faintest idea why.

    Nonfiction example: *Most people's biggest driving problem is getting their passengers to buckle up.* The best way to accomplish this life-saving task is to explain the facts.

6. QUESTION: The question hook asks a question that you intend to answer in the piece.

    Fiction example: *The problem for Jesse was this: what do you do with a large, purple dragon?* Hers landed in a meadow in front of her one Friday afternoon. Obviously Marlon had sent it, but she had no idea why.

    Nonfiction example: *Before you start the car, do you check to be certain all your passengers are buckled up?* You can save money, time, and grief with a two-second check.

7. STATEMENT OF AUTHORITY: The statement of authority hook is most often used by experts writing on their subjects of expertise. You can use it too, provided you show why you are an expert.

    Fiction example: *When Marlon sends you a purple dragon, he has a good reason.* I know. He sent me one, and it caused no end of trouble. (In this case the expert is Jesse.)

    Nonfiction example: *According to a survey I took of students in my school, only thirty percent of them buckle their seatbelts every time they get into a car.* They might buckle up more often if they knew the facts. (You are the expert because you did the survey.)

8. QUOTATION: The quotation hook begins with a quote from a real person or from a book, magazine, or newspaper. Just make sure it fits your story or subject. For fiction, you can make up books, magazines, or newspapers to quote.

    Fiction example: *"In 3050 King Fardmen declared the last dragon dead."—The History of the House of Fardmen.*
    Jesse had read the famous history of her country written by the scholar Quiliman, and she knew it was wrong, particularly on the subject of dragons. One Friday, over one hundred and fifty years after the king declared dragons extinct, a large purple dragon appeared before her. Dead? No. This dragon was most certainly alive, at least lively enough to cause her no end of trouble.

    Nonfiction example: *"I know I should wear seatbelts, but I often don't," said Bill Bramer, a student at Union College.* Bill is like many students at Union. Over seventy percent of those surveyed said they often fail to buckle their seatbelts.

9. STATISTICS: This statistics hook cites a statistic that leads into the piece.

   Fiction example: *According to the Fardmen Daily Screamer, over 80 percent of all dragon sightings in the year 4101 were somehow connected with one man, the magician named Marlon.* Experts claimed this statistic was pure twaddle. They maintained that both the Magician Marlon and dragons were myths. Jesse never believed in the magician, but the day a large, purple dragon appeared, she knew Marlon had sent it.

   Nonfiction example: *One in every eight people will be involved in an automobile accident at least once in their lives.* Even a minor fender-bender can produce serious injuries if the passengers are not wearing seatbelts.

10. COMPARISON OR CONTRAST: The comparison or contrast hook compares two things for similarities, contrasts their differences, or both.

    Fiction example: (Contrasting girls to dragons.) *Young, headstrong girls and dragons have little in common. Girls can rarely be successfully ordered around, whereas dragons are always under orders, usually those of a magician. Girls laugh at magicians; dragons worship them. Girls are sometimes pretty; dragons are always gorgeous, if you can ignore their stink.* Getting a girl together with a dragon is difficult, but this was the Magician Marlon's task one Friday when he sent a large, purple dragon to meet a girl named Jesse.

    Nonfiction example: (Contrasting the use of thirty seconds.) *It takes thirty seconds to buckle the average seatbelt and the same amount of time to die without one.* People who do not use seatbelts are twice as likely to die in an accident as those who do.

Additional Tips on Writing Leads

- You do not need to begin writing at the beginning of the piece. You may want to hold off writing the lead paragraph until you have written the rest of the piece—or at least until you have warmed up a little. On the other hand, some writers like to polish the lead before they write so much as an outline. It's up to you.

- If you aren't happy with your lead, try crossing out the first few sentences or paragraphs. Nine times out of ten, you will find a good strong lead somewhere in the first few paragraphs.

- Begin on a high point, even if it is not the beginning of the story. Don't be afraid to open with "Rich came to with his face pressed into the mud, a heavy boot on his neck." Then let Rich's thoughts explain how he got into this pickle. Be a bit careful, however. If you open with a combination hurricane, flood, and airplane crash, you may never be able to top your opening, and all stories need to build to a high point.

Springboard 8: Warm-ups for *Cold* Days

You don't start with any aesthetic manifesto, you just do what works.
—E. L. Doctorow

Writing does wax hot and cold. Like all other writers, you may sometimes have trouble starting because you are writing cold that day, so we have collected a list of warm-up ideas to help you get started on cold days. Don't be surprised by cold days; you will probably write cold about half the time. It doesn't mean that you shouldn't write that day. You should.

There is one curious aspect of writing cold that may interest you. Resistence may be uncomfortable for the writer, but it does not necessarily produce bad writing. In fact, some writers say that they produce their best work on cold days. Something in the feeling of pressing against resistance sharpens their concentration and slows them to a reasonable pace. Cold days aren't all bad. You, too, may grow to prefer them.

Try It

The next time you have a cold day, dig out the filesheet below and try one or more of the ideas listed on it. If you still feel cold, force yourself to write anyway.

WARM–UPS (FILESHEET)

- Concentrate on following your writer's routine. Don't worry about the deadline or the whole piece, just worry about the little part that you want to write today.

- Try to write badly. In her book, *Writing down the Bones*, Natalie Goldberg calls this composting. Gardeners compost old leaves and vegetable matter in order to prepare the garden soil. You are preparing to write the piece later by writing garbage now.

- Tell yourself that you will keep working for five more minutes. Then, if it's still going badly, you can try something else.

- Work on two pieces at the same time. If you are cold on one, switch to the other.

- Pick another section of the piece and start there. If you are stuck on the beginning, write the ending or the high point.

- Change your tools. Switch to a different pen. Try writing on a little bitty pad of paper. Try a great big pad with big bright pens. Type the story on a computer with the screen switched off. Tell your story to a tape recorder.

- Draw a picture of your story, then write about it.

- Edit and recopy a section you have already drafted.

- Try Braindancing and Downhilling, Zoom Lens, Between Friends, Hooks and Leaders, or Follow the Leader (pp. 74, 83, 78, 87 and 96).

- Hold a conference with your professor or a member of your writing group. Try to explain why you are having trouble and get their suggestions.

- Pretend that you are someone else writing on the same subject. If you are writing about a porcupine, pretend to be the porcupine. If you are writing a romance, pretend to be a Martian anthropologist writing a letter home explaining it.

- Write about whatever is in front of you. Close your eyes, turn your head, and open your eyes again. Describe whatever you see in detail. Then describe the things around it. Once you have warmed up, start writing your main piece using that description. For example, suppose you describe a crack in the linoleum as a warm-up. Go back to your main story and write a section where one of your characters is looking at a crack in the linoleum.

- Try writing your piece in a different genre. Write your essay as a song, your story as a how-to, your film script as a poem, your news article as a short story, or your personal experience as a letter.

- Braindance backward. Draw a pretty web of circles and lines without the thoughts filled in. Then go fill them in with whatever ideas seem appropriate.

- Forget that you are writing about anything. Just start writing and keep writing. Don't even try to write sentences. Write words or thoughts or feelings. Write a list of favorite words. Write nonsense. Just write anything at all.

- Write backward. Write the last sentence of a paragraph, then the sentence preceding it, then the sentence preceding that, working back to the beginning.

- Borrow a few words to start a first sentence.

EXAMPLE

I remember ...

You wouldn't think that ...

I have never ...

For the past two years, I ...

The last time I ...

If you have never ...

You think you know how to _____ until you ...

A good friend can ...

This morning was the first time I ...

If you are writing fiction, you may prefer to translate these sentence-starters into the third person past tense.

EXAMPLE

He (or she) remembered ...

He (or she) never dreamed that ...

He (or she) had never ...

- Make a connection to something totally unconnected and write about that. Suppose you are writing about the American Revolution. Look around you. How are things you see connected to the American Revolution? For example, how are your tennis shoes connected to the American Revolution. Come up with any old idea on how they might be connected, and use your connection as a first sentence of a warm-up paragraph or two. Go ahead! Be ridiculous.

EXAMPLE

How are tennis shoes connected to the American Revolution?

The tennis shoe was invented to help Daniel Boone cross the Cumberland Gap.

EXAMPLE

How are fluorescent lights connected to the American Revolution?

Ben Franklin snapped on the fluorescent light and then ...

- Make up a starter sentence. Fold a piece of paper in half lengthwise. On the first half write a list of subjects (human, animal, vegetable, mineral, or any other noun). On the second half write a list of unusual verbs. A thesaurus or a dictionary can suggest words. (Don't be afraid to choose verbs you don't yet know; just be sure to look them up.) Open the paper, so that the subjects and the verbs are lined up. Write a sentence using the subject and the verb on a given line. Write about anything the sentence suggests.

EXAMPLE

handwriting	grumble
anteaters	joust
loneliness	poise

My *handwriting grumbles* onto the page.

Each night, *anteaters joust* with a thousand prey.

Loneliness poised on my doorstep.

Springboard 9: Follow the Leader

The instruction we find in books is like fire. We fetch it from our neighbors, kindle it at home, communicate it to others, and it becomes the property of all.

—Voltaire

In his wonderful book *100 Ways to Improve Your Writing*, Gary Provost points out that writing is creating music with words. Teaching yourself to write is much like teaching yourself to sing: a lot of learning is done just by singing along. "Follow the Leader" is not so much one activity as an all purpose method for learning just about anything you wish on writing. It's simple. Find an example of what you want to learn, study it, then write your own versions until you have a feel for it. Don't try to imitate the style of the writer. It will sound odd. Just write along similar lines using your own words and your own ideas.

EXAMPLE

Suppose you are studying punctuation rules and you run across something like this:

"Place a comma after subordinate clauses beginning a sentence.
-After she finished her homework, she went to the party.

-Because the elephant population has grown, the parkland has slowly been denuded of trees."

Understanding the rule is difficult, especially if you can't remember what a subordinate clause is. On the other hand, writing your own versions of the examples follow-the-leader style is easy.

Model: After she finished her homework, she went to the party.

Own versions: After Bob finished mowing the lawn, he took a nap.

After he jumped a tall building, Superman flew home.

After Marie read the report, she rewrote it.

It doesn't take long to develop a feel for the rule, even though you still don't know what a subordinate clause is. Once you have practiced a few versions, you may want to understand the rule. Check through the index to find the definition of subordinate clause. You may have read that definition before, but this time, it starts to make sense. (It is a clause beginning with after, before, if, because, since, when and other such subordinating words. Like all clauses, a subordinating clause contains a subject and a verb. Unlike main clauses, a subordinate clause cannot stand alone as a complete sentence.) Later on, you will find yourself automatically placing the comma after the subordinate clause when you write—even if you don't remember the actual rule. It just sounds right and looks right to you.

You can use Follow the Leader to learn any writing concept; for example, what is a paragraph. Choose some good paragraphs and write your own versions using the same type of structure and organization until you have a good feel for how a paragraph flows together.

You can also use Follow the Leader to learn any style rule. For example, in books on style you'll often read: "Use the active voice." In other words, change "The book was written by the professor" to "The professor wrote the book." What is the active voice? Study the examples and practice writing your own versions changing sentences to the active voice:

Model: The book was written by the professor. The professor wrote the book.

Own Versions:

The book was eaten by the puppy.	The puppy ate the book.
The game was played by amateurs.	Amateurs played a game.
A speech was given by Sue.	Sue gave a speech.

You can also learn how to structure and organize pieces of writing with Follow the Leader. Choose a well-organized piece and outline it. Then write your own version using the outline.

The possible uses of Follow the Leader are limited only by your imagination. Use it to study your favorite authors. How did he or she put together that wonderful description of a boat? Use it to discover how to satisfy your professors. How is the example of a good paper organized? What types of information work best? Regular use of Follow the Leader in your practice journal will produce spectacular improvements in your writing. We guarantee it.

Try It

We have a reason for presenting Follow the Leader at this point. In the next chapter we cover a series of techniques to help you make your writing sound more stylish, more professional. You can learn every one of them with Follow the Leader.

Try this now. First choose a writing idea. It can be fiction or nonfiction. If you choose a nonfiction idea, be sure to choose a familiar subject so that you won't need to do a lot of research. Once you have an idea, turn to chapter 4 and choose any one of the techniques. (They are organized alphabetically.) This first time, we recommend choosing *action* or *description* if you are using a fiction idea, *examples* or *anecdotes* if you are using a non-fiction idea. Copy the example from chapter 4 at the top of the page, then write your own version around your writing idea modelling it after the example.

EXAMPLE (using action) — *Writing Idea:* A story about a woman lost in an airport in a foreign country.

Model from chapter 4 (the action is italicized):

"You will go." *The milk-eyes looked through him to the sea, to the snow, to the line of blue that was the sky.* "You will go now."

> And there was such strength in his voice that Rusel knew he must go. *He took the handlebar in one hand and pulled the hook, and the dogs surged away and Rusel let them run without looking back.*
>
> — Gary Paulsen, *Dogsong*

Own version:

> "Oui, madame?" *The old man smiled placing his hand on her arm.* "Puis-je vous aidez?"
>
> He seemed ready to help, whatever he was saying. He was the first person who had smiled at her all day. *She dug into her purse for her phrase book, scattering maps and schedules in her rush to communicate with a friendly face.*

As you can see, our version only resembles the original model in that we used action to write our little scene in the same way Gary Paulsen used action to write his. This is important. You never want to copy another writer's words and call them your own. That's plagiarism. Not only will plagiarism earn you a well-deserved *F* or a trip to court, it isn't fair to other writers to steal their work. You would not want people to steal yours. On the other hand, modelling your writing after good writing or even copying good writing in order to learn how to do something only makes sense.

When you use Follow the Leader, be careful not to plagiarize. If your own version turns out to be as different from the model as in our example, don't worry about it. Being inspired by another writer is not plagiarism. If your own version turns out suspiciously close to the model, keep it in your practice journal and mark it "modelled after...." Keep anything you copy directly in your practice journal for your eyes only. Be sure to note prominently that it is a copy for learning purposes only, so that you don't later accidentally use it thinking it is your own.

Student's Notebook:
On Preconceptions

When we talk to students about writing, they tend to list all of the things they can't do. "I don't understand commas;" "I can't organize the structure;" "My sentences are always wrong;" "I use too many words." What these students are really doing is translating a comment on one piece into a sweeping generalization about their abilities to write. They have long since forgotten who made the comment. It could very well have been someone who knew little about writing. They have forgotten the context of the comment. Just because a teacher wrote "wordy" on one piece does not mean the writer is wordy in every piece.

Set aside any preconceptions you now hold about your writing ability. Don't let vague anxieties about old grammar mistakes, half-remembered punctuation rules, or confusing comments trail around after you. This outdated mental baggage only spoils your confidence; it doesn't help you write. It doesn't matter if your spelling is good or bad, if you know the rules of punctuation or not. Many students believe that they can write nonfiction fairly well but aren't creative enough for fiction. Baloney. Most students have not written enough fiction to know. The truth is, you don't know how well you write, and you never will. Each new piece is a new adventure. You may produce something terrific this time or not. But even poor results do not mean that you are a bad writer. Professionals throw away plenty of drafts and don't think much of writing three or four drafts to get a useable "rough draft." They don't equate the need to rewrite with failure. They try again.

If anxiety about your writing ability or some aspect of writing makes you stumble, define specifically what causes your anxiety, then take action. You don't understand commas? Buy a good book on punctuation and relearn the rules. You can't organize. Study past work. Outline it. Where does the organization fall apart? Why? How could you have reorganized it? Make sure you understand the mistake, the rule, or the comment and how to correct the problem.

Keep in mind that not everyone who sees your work is competent. They make mistakes, too, and could have told you the wrong thing. If you cannot really remember the problem, forget it. You can always catch it the next time you bump into it. In the meantime, do not let worry about such things keep you from writing with confidence and enthusiasm.

Chapter 4

Writing with Style

If you're a singer, you lose your voice. A baseball player loses his arm. A writer gets more knowledge, and if he's good, the older he gets the better he writes.

— Mickey Spillane

INTRODUCTION

Most beginners long to write with more style. "How do I make it sound better?" they ask in every writing class. The question of style is frustrating. Often, the harder one tries to sound stylish, the worse the result. Each person has a writing voice as distinctive as a singing voice. The authentic ring of the writer's natural voice is one of the things that separates good writing from bad. When one tries to imitate the style of another writer or just to sound "formal" or "funny," it is like imitating an opera star. Your own voice sounds honest, if rough; the imitation sounds absurd.

We suggest that you never try to sound stylish or to imitate the style of other writers. Write simply and honestly in your own words. Improve the sound of your work by learning *technique*. We use the term technique loosely. A technique can be almost anything: a rule of punctuation, tips on writing dialogue, a concept such as knowing what a scene is, a writing rule, or suggestions for perking up sentences. Every time you ask "how can I...," you want to know a technique. Every experienced writer has a whole bag of them to use for solving problems. Instead of trying to sound good, concentrate on building your supply of techniques. Think about how to solve a writing problem, rather than about how you might sound. And be patient. You won't improve your style overnight.

This chapter is organized as a mini-dictionary of techniques because technical questions pop up all through the writing process, and, unfortunately, answers don't pop to mind so easily. Each entry has a section explaining the technique along with examples you can use for Follow the Leader (see Springboard 9, chapter 3). The "Tricks of the Trade" contain further tips, especially those which may help you revise. It will help you learn to revise your work (see chapter 5) if you write a sample, then consult the Tricks of the Trade and rewrite your sample incorporating some of the tricks.

Before you tackle *action* or *anecdotes*, skip back to the explanations of *scenes* and *sections*. Amateurs tend to think and organize in paragraphs; professionals think in fictional scenes and nonfiction sections. Why? It's easier. The paragraph is a slippery devil. It may be one sentence long. It may have a main point and subpoints, but not necessarily. Some paragraphs are short, just to give the reader a breather. The scene or section, on the other hand, has a fairly clearcut goal. It can be one paragraph long or several pages, but the goal won't change. Follow the professionals' lead. Start writing one scene or one section at a time, and let the paragraphs fall where they may. Your style will improve, and so will your sanity.

One thing you may not realize is that the distinction between fiction and nonfiction starts to break down at the level of technique. Action and description may be more prominent in fiction, but nonfiction writers use both quite often. We've roughly identified the techniques as fiction and nonfiction, but don't take that too seriously. It may be easier to learn, say, description from practicing a fictional description, but that doesn't mean that you won't later use what you've learned in a nonfiction piece. You will.

Finally, this dictionary of techniques does not cover every possible technique. There are thousands of techniques, and each writer carries around a little bit different bag of tricks. These will help you start your own collection. It's up to you to add to it any technique that helps you write.

ACTION

Explanation

Action is what the characters do in a scene, as opposed to *dialogue*, which is what characters say. Action can include big actions (e.g., "Alex jumped from the shed roof to the garden walk and ran to the front of the house") or little actions, sometimes called business (e.g., "Alex set his glass on the counter"). Too much action is hard to follow, so action is almost always woven together with dialogue, introspection, description, or narrative (see later entries).

EXAMPLE

> "You will go." *The milk-eyes looked through him to the sea, to the snow, to the line of blue that was the sky.* "You will go now."
> And there was such strength in his voice that Rusel knew he must go. *He took the handlebar in one hand and pulled the hook, and the dogs surged away and Rusel let them run without looking back.*
> —Gary Paulsen, *Dogsong*

EXAMPLE

> "Hullo," he said, beaming. "Where did you spring from? Come and have a warmer up at the Angel."
> *I nodded and walked beside him, shuffling on the thawing remains of the previous week's snow.*
> —Dick Francis, *Flying Finish*

Tricks of the Trade

- Your reader must be able to picture who is coming into and going out of the scene and what the characters are doing. A little bit of business adds color and a sense of a real scene. But readers have good imaginations; you don't need to write down every move your characters make.

- Beginners often try to add zip by adding adverbs: "He walked quickly and quietly from the room." But adverbs slow the action down. If you want to slow it down, fine. If you want to speed it up, use a good strong verb: "He tiptoed from the room." Below is a starter list of strong verbs:

Walked Quickly		*Walked Slowly*	
dashed	hopped	wandered	dawdled
raced	roared	sauntered	toured
ran	jogged	strolled	traversed
darted	scampered	ambled	hiked
bolted	skittered	rambled	straggled
tore	loped	meandered	limped
jaunted	gallivanted	moseyed	drifted
hastened	scurried	roamed	shuffled
speeded	careened	hobbled	prowled
hurried	skipped	roved	trekked
rushed	fled	crawled	scuttled
escaped	scrambled	staggered	limped
flitted	bounced	toddled	inched
jumped	blasted	wobbled	teetered

- If the strong verbs don't seem strong enough, try an unusual verb. "He whispered away." "She screamed into the driveway."

- *Suddenly.* What to do with all those suddenlies? Because it's an adverb, suddenly slows down the action just as it should speed it up. Try crossing it out. Or try to foreshadow it.

EXAMPLE

Change—

Richard spread the newspaper on the dining room table. Suddenly, the tarantula pounced.

to—

Richard flushed away the crumbled tissue and the spider. Big spider, he chuckled. Maria wouldn't know a big spider. Some people were really funny about spiders. Now in Nam, those were big spiders.
He spread the newspaper on the dining room table and settled down to check the stock prices. Not that he owned stocks anymore. It was a habit he couldn't break, something from childhood, like making the bed or cleaning the table after dinner. The day seemed off-color without it. *He glimpsed a furry leg before he saw the tarantula.* Later, all he could remember was two intense spider eyes perched on top of two huge fangs.

ANECDOTES

Explanation

When writers present examples, they sometimes write them as thumbnail stories called *anecdotes*. People like reading stories, even pint-sized stories. Anecdotes written with fiction techniques, such as dialogue or action, are sometimes called fictional anecdotes, but the facts of the little story are real. Some short magazine articles are all anecdotes, nothing else.

EXAMPLE

> *When Rasila decided to buy a dog, she spent several hours debating which set of floppy ears and brown eyes seemed most appealing before a smart pet store owner set her straight. Selecting the breed to match the owner's lifestyle is important, he explained, because personality traits bred into a dog cannot be trained out of it.*

EXAMPLE

> Writers become attached to their pens. My favorite word weapon is the cheap cartridge fountain pen. The cheap ones are better than the expensive ones, incidentally. They flow more easily with the ideas. The only problem is replacing them when they gum up. *I spent four hours tracking one down yesterday. I finally found one—just one—buried at the bottom of a rack of designer felt tips and ball points. Ominously, some of the stores no longer carry fountain pens.* If the cheap fountain pen follows the dinosaur into extinction, I may be next.

Tricks of the Trade

- Anecdotes must be short and punchy. Try the three-sentence technique: the first sets up the story, the second contains a crisis, the third leads into the next section with a solution. Television advertisements use this constantly.

EXAMPLE

First sentence setup:	"I could never get grass stains out of the children's clothes."
Second sentence crisis:	"One day Jimmy's teacher sent him home from school to get a clean shirt."
Third sentence solution:	"Then I discovered Super Sudso Detergent."
Next sentence:	"Yessiree, folks, Super Sudso gets out the toughest stains."

(A word of warning: When you use the three-sentence technique, make sure it doesn't sound like you are selling slicers and dicers for $29.95.)

DESCRIPTION
Explanation

When you tell a story, you want your reader to be able to picture the story. Just writing what your characters say and do isn't enough. "Don't jump!" yelled John. Is John standing on top of a mountain or in a schoolyard? Is John young or old, skinny or fat, tall or short? Remember that reading is more like listening to the radio than watching television. Readers can't imagine what a scene or a character looks like without being told. Use *description* to show the reader what the setting and the characters look like.

EXAMPLE

Tim Archer got into the utility and drove it from the Banbury Feed and General Supply Pty Ltd, down the main street of the town. *The car was a 1946 Chevrolet, somewhat battered by four years of station use, a sturdy practical vehicle with a coupe front seat and an open truck body behind. In this rear portion he was carrying a forty-four gallon drum of Diesel oil, four reels of barbed wire, a can of kerosene, a sack of potatoes, a coil of new sisal rope, a carton of groceries, and a miscellaneous assortment of spades and jacks and chains that seldom left the truck.*

—Nevil Shute, *A Far Country*

Description often does double duty. It describes and tells the story at the same time. Even though Shute is describing a truck, his reader learns a lot about Tim Archer. He's clearly a farmer, but the word station tips us off that the story is set in Australia, and the 1946 Chevrolet lets us know the story takes place after World War II.

Tricks of the Trade

• The trick to writing good description is details. Look how many Shute uses, all of them small. Don't describe everything, just describe a few good details. Use "Zoom Lens" (p. 83) to help you choose details.

• Try the *background-middleground-foreground* method of choosing details. Imagine the scene as a picture. Pick a detail on the horizon, a detail in the middle of the picture, and finally, a detail right up close.

EXAMPLE

Background—tractor dust; *middleground*—elm; *foreground*—shovel and tricycle

The dust from a tractor floated along the horizon, and cicadas sang in the huge elm next to the barn. A battered shovel lay on the lawn next to a shiny new tricycle.

You could also reverse the order, describing the shovel then the elm, and finally the tractor.

EXAMPLE

> A battered shovel lay on the lawn next to a shiny new tricycle. The cicadas sang in the huge elm next to the barn, and dust from a tractor floated along the horizon.

Adjectives add to description, but too many make it dull. Instead of adding adjectives, use less abstract words. The abstraction ladder helps writers remember the specific words they know. The top rung of the ladder contains the most general words; each rung below that contains more and more specific words. On the bottom rung, write the specific word you've chosen. If you wish, add a short adjective.

EXAMPLE

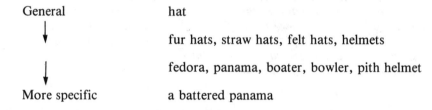

General	hat
	fur hats, straw hats, felt hats, helmets
	fedora, panama, boater, bowler, pith helmet
More specific	a battered panama

EXAMPLE

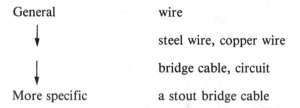

General	wire
	steel wire, copper wire
	bridge cable, circuit
More specific	a stout bridge cable

Use a thesaurus, synonym finder, or *What's What* to help you write abstraction ladders.

DIALOGUE

Explanation

Dialogue shows what characters say, just as action shows what they do.

EXAMPLE

> Jason dashed through the kitchen, slammed the door behind him and arrived panting in the living room. His sister, Mary, was curled up in the big chair reading a book.

"What do you want?" she asked irritably.

"Oh," Jason replied, glancing over his shoulder, *"nothing really."*

Mary glared at him. *"Don't bug me then."*

"I wasn't. I just…"

"You were too. You are always bugging me." Mary flounced from the room, leaving Jason with his problem unsolved.

Dialogue sounds as if real people were talking, but it is not written exactly as people talk. That would be dull.

EXAMPLE

"Hi," said Jane.

"Hi," answered Sue.

"Where are you going?" asked Jane.

"English class. I'm not ready for the test."

"Me too."

"I have to go to my locker first."

In dialogue, this conversation is squeezed together and laced with action.

Jane caught up with Sue in the hallway. "Hi. Where are you off to in such a hurry?"

"English class," groaned Sue, "and I'm not ready for the test. Better get my notes from my locker."

"You'll be late," warned Jane.

"'Tis far, far better to be late than to flunk."

Tricks of the Trade

- Pay some attention to making your dialogue sound like your characters. A cab driver in New York and a cowboy in Arizona do not speak the same way. On the other hand, don't be silly, putting in "howdy pardner" or "New Yoik." One subtle word or phrase here and there can be quite effective.

- Make sure your reader knows who is speaking. When you write dialogue, start a new paragraph each time a different character speaks. Be sure to say "so-and-so said" if the alternating paragraphs don't make it clear who is speaking.

- Instead of using the word *said*, you can use action to indicate who is speaking. *Said* is usually fine, but you can add emotion or action by using an alternate word for *said*. (Don't overdo it; said is best most of the time.) On page 108 is a starter list.

answered	fumed	remarked
asserted	giggled	repeated
babbled	glared	replied
badgered	grieved	responded
bellowed	grinned	retorted
blathered	grumbled	roared
blurted	guessed	screamed
brayed	hollered	shouted
bristled	lamented	sighed
cackled	laughed	snickered
chafed	mimicked	sniggered
chatted	moaned	sniped
chattered	moped	sobbed
cheered	mourned	speculated
chided	murmured	spouted
chortled	nagged	squalled
chuckled	nettled	stewed
claimed	noted	stopped
cried	paused	stormed
croaked	pestered	tittered
crowed	pointed out	wailed
declared	predicted	whined
demanded	promised	whispered
explained	queried	whooped
exploded	raged	worried
fretted	rambled on	yelped

EXAMPLES

Explanation

Examples are the life of the nonfiction party. They make dull ideas come alive. "Not all beautiful trees make good street trees" is pretty ho-hum without examples.

EXAMPLE

> Not all beautiful trees make good street trees. *The London plane's iron roots can shred a cement sidewalk or snap a steel water main. Dutch elm disease has nearly wiped out the elm, a popular street tree at the turn of the century. Street trees can't be maintenance headaches or prone to disease. They must grow quickly to a size that can withstand car exhaust and petty vandalism. Their branches should not bat pedestrians in the face or rain sticky sap on parked cars.* That's a lot to ask of a tree.

You can string examples together, as above, or you can use one good example to make your point:

EXAMPLE

> Not all beautiful trees make good street trees. *At the turn of the century, elm trees were planted along boulevards and city squares in towns all across the United States. In the 1960s Dutch elm disease—a virus that infects and kills elms—began to spread from east to west stripping city after city of its elegant elms. In the 1980s it picked Denver's boulevards clean and pushed on towards San Francisco.*

Tricks of the Trade

- Deciding on how you want to present your example(s) will help you write your section. Think of your examples in three ways: the short example, the extended example, and the story-like example.

  short: "Elms are killed by Dutch elm disease."

  extended: "Elms are killed by Dutch elm disease. By the 1980s, this virus destroyed many of the elms in the United States."

  story-like: see last example of street trees above.

- You can use two or three long examples. If, however, you have told a story in the first example that you use, be sure to tell stories of about the same length for the other examples. Otherwise, the later examples will seem incomplete and tacked on.

- Keep the same kinds of examples together. All the examples in the first paragraph illustrate the point, but the examples include specific trees, bad characteristics, and good characteristics. They are presented in groups.

- One specialized example is the list. It's used in textbooks and reference books to quickly present a large number of examples in a way that's easy to read.

EXAMPLE

Not all beautiful trees make good street trees. City aborists should not include the following trees on their lists of approved trees:

elms

London planes

large pines with heavy sap

weeping willows

Introduce examples with *for example* or *such as* if it might not be clear to your reader that you are giving an example.

EXAMPLES

Not all beautiful trees make good street trees. The elm, *for example*, is gorgeous, but a poor choice for a street tree.

Trees *such as* the elm, the London plane, and the weeping willow, should not be used for street tree plantings.

- To present quick examples you can use *e.g.* (e.g., this is an example of how to use e.g.). It comes from the Latin *exempli gratis* which means "for example." Punctuate it the same way as you would *for example* by setting it off with commas. You don't need to put your example in parentheses, but the parentheses can help readers who can't remember what e.g. means to figure out that the part in parentheses is an example. Be a bit careful with e.g. Use it only when you need to be brief and it won't put the reader off. Generally a few e.g.'s help academic pieces, serious how-to pieces, and textbooks because they allow for more examples than the writer could otherwise present without interrupting the flow of the ideas. Avoid e.g. in fiction, popular articles, or interoffice memos where few readers will know what it means.

FLASHBACK

Explanation

Writers don't like to begin at the beginning. They like to start stories or chapters with a high point, not background. After they have the reader's attention, they use *flashback* to fill in the background from an earlier time.

EXAMPLE

Jim Baker swore Dannie would never drag him out for another vacation. He urged the ancient horse along, but it was determined to storm the mountain one aching step at a time.

"Isn't this fun?" laughed Dannie. She guided her elderly mare alongside Jim's horse.

"Great fun for an interior decorator from Manhattan maybe," thought Jim. *He remembered the time his best friend Bob had signed them both up to ride the broncs in the Alamosa Days Rodeo. They were both just kids, but Bob's dad was a rancher and put a high price on horsemanship...*

Tricks of the Trade

• Flashback is a useful tool, but getting into and out of a flashback can be a bit tricky. Most stories are written in past tense, to the first sentence of the flashback must use *had* (had signed, had gone, had flown, had begun, etc.). It's best to use *remembered, recalled, thought back,* or *reminisced about the time* to introduce the flashback.

The easiest way to get out of the flashback and back to the story is to have a character from the present scene, such as Dannie, say something. ("Oh look! A deer!" cried Dannie.) Action also works. (Jim's horse halted abruptly.) Avoid introspection, description, or narrative. They can be used, but it's easy to confuse your reader.

FORESHADOWING
Explanation

Sometimes you need to hint at something that is going to happen later in the story to *foreshadow* what will happen.

Foreshadowing builds suspense. It also helps you plant clues in mysteries, provide future escapes for trapped adventurers, and other handy necessities. In the nineteenth century, writers would foreshadow with sentences such as "little did she know that buying an apple could ruin her life forever." Today such foreshadowing is thought heavy-handed, but the idea is the same.

Suppose you are planning later in your story to trap your hero in the bedroom of an old house. Most bedrooms have windows. Why doesn't your hero escape through the window? You could say there are no windows, and your reader would reply, "how terribly inconvenient for the writer." Try foreshadowing a reason why the window won't work. For example, early in the story, a character can wash the window and comment on what a long way it is to the ground from that bedroom window. You can make the window into a French door and have a character accidentally drop the key to the door down a heating vent. Your imagination is the only limit.

You can also plant clues in mysteries with foreshadowing. In your story, if Detective Snoop desperately searches the mug books all morning, then just happens to pick up the criminal's wallet on the street while he's on his way to the coffee shop, the coincidence is too convenient. But suppose back in the beginning of the story, Detective Snoop's neighbor drops by to return some sugar, hands him a wallet that she found on the bus, and asks him to take it to the lost and found. Snoop throws it in his glove compartment and forgets it. Then, when he's desperately searching the mug books, he can remember the wallet when he sees a familiar face. Much better.

Tricks of the Trade

- Remember, you don't need to write the story in order. If you find that you need some foreshadowing earlier in the story, go back and insert it at the appropriate point.

INTROSPECTION
Explanation

Introspection shows the reader what your characters think. You can present the thoughts of characters using either *introspection* or *internal dialogue*.

EXAMPLE

Introspection

Allen raced to the bus stop. *He couldn't be late again. It was the third time — and that could only mean detention. Mom wasn't going to understand...*

Internal Dialogue

Allen raced to the bus stop. *Oh no, he thought. I can't be late again. It's my third time. I'll get detention. I don't think Mom's going to understand...*

Tricks of the Trade

- To save your reader confusion, stick with the point of view of one character all through the scene. Don't switch from the thoughts of one character to the thoughts of another.

- To move out of introspection and back into the scene, use the flashback reentry technique: interrupt the character's thoughts with dialogue or action from the scene.

NARRATIVE
Explanation

Narrative <u>*tells*</u> the story, whereas *dialogue, action, introspection,* and *description* <u>*show*</u> the story. In nonfiction, narrative also tells about the idea, whereas examples, anecdotes, and description show the idea.

Narrative is essential. Even "Show, Don't Tell" can be overdone, and narrative moves the story along. Nothing, however, is duller than long paragraphs of narrative, even well-written narrative. Use narrative for a purpose, keep it brief, and practice writing richer narrative.

Beginners often write their first stories entirely in narrative:

EXAMPLE

> Then Bill decided to leave India, so he got on a train and went to Nepal. In Kathmandu he met a man in a white suit. Bill thought the man was bad, so he called his boss in America and asked him what to do. Then...

> *or*

> Fort Sumter is in Charleston Harbor, South Carolina. It's important because the first shots in the Civil War were fired there in 1861.

There is nothing wrong with a good simple narrative sentence, but consider making it into a scene. If it's not important enough to become a scene, try enriching the narrative with a little description, action, or dialogue. First write a few simple narrative sentences. Don't use *go* or *went*. Be specific about what happened:

EXAMPLE

> Bill got on the train at the Calcutta station. Four days later, he arrived in Nepal. When he got off the train, he was greeted by a man in a white suit.

Once you have done this, rewrite these sentences enriching them with more detail.

EXAMPLE

> When Bill finally climbed the steps to the Calcutta train station, the platform was packed with a thousand people, shouting and pushing. They shoved battered suitcases and curious parcels into one another's backs as they fought to reach seats close to the open windows but far from the locomotive's engines. After a twenty-minute struggle, he finally wedged himself into an aisle seat near the center of

the train. Four days later, he stepped off an elderly bus onto the streets of Kathmandu. With his first breath of cool mountain air, all thought of steamy, crowded Calcutta slipped away.

"Welcome, Mr. Mendal," said a voice behind him.

Bill turned. The speaker was an odd little man in an impeccable white suit.

You can also enrich nonfiction narrative, although you needn't get carried away. Enrich it with a few more facts, a little description, a tiny anecdote.

EXAMPLE

The city of Charleston, S.C. is a city of azaleas and graceful colonial homes. Before the Civil War, its busy harbor was the major southern port for shipping tobacco and textiles to the wealthy in England and the home of Fort Sumter. Believing that Fort Sumter gave the North a bird's-eye view of one of the South's most precious trade links, Southern Confederates surrounded the fort on April 2, 1861 and ordered its commander to surrender. When he refused, they fired on the fort, and the Civil War began.

Tricks of the Trade

- Use your encyclopedia and a good atlas to learn details. Moving a character from one exotic place to another is a wonderful way to learn about world geography and map reading. Because narrative moves so quickly, it requires more research than other parts of the story.

For the passage about Calcutta, we used an atlas to discover, for example, that there is no train from Calcutta to Nepal. The train stops at Monghyr, about 200 miles from Kathmandu, the capital of Nepal, and the trip would have to be finished by bus. Using our compass, we measured about 700 miles by train and road from Calcutta to Kathmandu. With delays or irregular bus service, we guessed that might take four days. Kathmandu (population 395,000) is the only place in Nepal large enough to be likely to have regular bus service. From our desk encyclopedia, we learned that Calcutta is the oldest, most overcrowded city in India (population 9,000,000 people). It is extremely hot and humid by contrast to Kathmandu, which is in a high mountain valley with temperatures often below freezing

We could have gone further and found out for sure if the train from Calcutta to Monghyr was diesel or steam, what the passenger cars look like, exactly how long such a trip might take, etc. We might have tried to discover what the weather would be like in both cities during a certain month of the year.

The need for realistic facts to write the story makes pursuing the facts a pleasure. Conduct a little treasure hunt. Use your imagination for research. It's a fun way to learn. Writing a paragraph about steamy, crowded Calcutta and crisp, cool Kathmandu will make your geography memorable for many years. You may never forget that there is no train from Calcutta to Kathmandu.

Research can also enrich nonfiction. There are whole books written about Charleston and Fort Sumter, but an encyclopedia and other reference books can help you find just a few extra details to draw a better picture of graceful Charleston and to depict the opening shot of the war. Use the facts to help you enrich your writing; don't copy them.

- Use words such as *told, explained, went, came,* and *left* in narration to cut out repetitive dialogue or action.

EXAMPLES

Mary told Priscilla about the ghost

Mike went to the store. He wasn't gone long, but when he got home...

- Somewhere along the line, someone is going to tell you never to use *I* or *we* in nonfiction. This is not necessarily good advice. Some types of nonfiction, such as personal experience, need *I* or *we*. What you shouldn't do is intrude on your narrative with "I think" or "we believe." Just tell the story or make your point. The whole piece is what you think; you don't need to say it. The trick to writing warm, friendly nonfiction is to go ahead and write your draft using *I* or, if you are coauthoring, *we*. Then go back and cut any *I* or *we* that you don't need. If you are not coauthoring, don't use *we* at all. You'll sound like an old-fashioned nurse: "We must take our medicine now, mustn't we?"

RULES ON "WRITING RULES"

Explanation

Every writing technique, from scene construction to punctuation, has an accompanying set of rules. While these guides are a big help to experienced writers, they often cause more harm than good to beginners.

Professionals don't treat writing rules the same way that novices do. Professionals look on rules as ideas to be tested, not laws to be obeyed. Knowing what good writing is, they will cheerfully break a rule to improve the writing and happily attack any copy editor who tries to change the decision. They also have enough experience to know the full rule, not an oversimplified version of it. For example, students are often told: "Don't repeat words." The full rule is: "Vary your words within reason, but deliberately repeat key words for transition, emphasis, and unity"—a very different rule. Working writers also know which rules take priority over others, something students do not.

Because writing rules are so pervasive and so often misused, a few rules on rules may help you:

1. Go easy on the rules. The secret to good writing is not to overdo anything, including the rules. Treat the rules as rules of thumb. Always prefer good writing to following a rule. And if you feel paralyzed by a rule, forget about it. It's more important to write than to worry about rules.

2. Use your judgment. Remember, nobody knows all the rules—not your professors, not your smart roommate, not a hot novelist, not even Shakespeare. Don't follow rules because other people suggest it unless you feel it improves the result.

3. Some rules are more important than others. They should always come first:

   - *Be clear.* If your reader can't understand you, nothing else makes a bit of difference.

   - *Enjoy your own work.* If you would not want to read it, why should other people?

   - *Care about your reader.* How lucky you are that another person has taken the time to read what you wrote. Don't try to impress your reader; try to take care of your reader. Make it easy to read, and put your whole self into it. Write with enthusiasm. Make it something special.

   - *Be honest.* Don't pad, don't plagiarize, and don't try to sound fancy or important. Give your own point of view in your own words.

   - *Make up your own rules.* If you find something that helps you write, record it in your personal journal. Your own rules are the most important rules. They are especially designed to help *you.*

Tricks of the Trade

- We prefer advising people what to try rather than what not to do. But a few no's help, too. Don't follow the rules below even though you hear other students recommend them. They are the mark of the amateur. They appear so frequently in student papers that professors and others can pick them out at forty paces as the products of rules in the embarrassing *Student Manual of Bad Style*:

  Big-Word-Babble. Use every word you can remember and make your sentences sound fancy. Changing simple verbs such as *use* into complicated ones such as *utilize* is a favorite tactic of the big word babblers. (Wow, we're impressed!) Some babblers choose a few good vocabulary words from the thesaurus and toss them in at random. Some get so caught up that they forget the sentences and end up simply stringing together all the big words they know. All big word babblers tend to forget to say something interesting to a reader. Big word babble is all sound, no meaning.

Give-'Em-What-They-Like Syndrome. Just sprinkle in a few *howevers, in conclusions,* and *moreovers.* Be sure to include a *thus* and *therefore* to keep the professor happy. Tack *more research is required* as the last sentence on every paper. The give-em-what-they-like fan is never concerned about using *moreover* to help the reader understand, only with fitting the word in somewhere. Again, saying something is secondary.

Make-It-Look-Good Syndrome. Type it up. Throw in some footnotes. Don't run over or under the page limit by so much as a word, even if you must chop off the end to do it. The alternate version is to pad everything, churning out five pages of useless fluff for every page of clear writing, all saying nothing.

Copy-the-Encyclopedia Syndrome. Just copy it out of the encyclopedia to make it sound good. Change a few words here and there to make it your own. Many students don't even check if the borrowed section makes any sense in context. It sounds good, and that's all these plagiarists want.

Don't. You are better than this.

SCENES

Explanation

One of the things that will help your writing sound more professional is to practice writing one scene at a time. A *scene* is just a small section of the story. Think of it as a little story within your bigger story.

There are two ways you can present the story. You could write a simple sentence telling the plot: "John went to the old house where he met a man who told him about a buried treasure." (Don't let the word "plot" worry you. As Paul Darcy Boles says, "...all Plot has ever meant is *What happens first* and then *What happens next.*")

The little sentences of plot tell the story, but a whole story told this way becomes a boring list of what happened first, then what happened next. You could also write this part of the plot as a scene. A scene doesn't just tell the story, it *shows* the story.

EXAMPLE

The house was easy enough to find. It was an ancient Victorian sitting in the middle of a spanking new suburban development. Huge trees and a weedy gravel driveway marked it as the farmhouse that once presided over the fields now turned into tidy lawns and matching driveways. A television blared from behind the screen door.

"Mr. Hatford?" asked John through the screen.

"Go away!" shouted a voice.

"Maureen sent me. She couldn't get off work. You said it was urgent."

The sound of the game show snapped off, and an elderly man shuffled to the door.

"Who are you?" Hatford hooked the door closed.

"A friend of Maureen's."

"A lawyer?"

"No."

"One of them banker boyfriends of hers?"

John grinned. "No actually, I ... I guess you could say I'm unemployed."

"Oh well, that's okay then," Hatford unlatched the door and motioned John in. "I keep telling Maureen that we gotta be careful. She's just too trusting, that girl. One of these days, she'll have trouble."

To write a scene, the writer weaves description, dialogue, action, introspection, and narrative together like threads in a braid. These are sometimes called the fiction tools, although they are often used in nonfiction as well. Here's a list:

Description: describes the setting or the characters

Dialogue: what the characters say

Action: what the characters do

Introspection: what the characters think

Narrative: what happened in a simple sentence (telling the story instead of showing it)

See other entries in this chapter for more detail on each of these.

Tricks of the Trade

- Not every part of the story is told in scenes, just the most important parts. The next time you are reading a story or a novel, see if you can pick out the scenes. When you choose which parts of your story to write as scenes, start with important scenes that move the story forward.

- Don't pack too much plot into a scene. Most scenes take place in one setting with a certain set of characters. If too much happens, the scene becomes too long. It sometimes helps to write the scene as one or two narrative sentences, like we did with John and Mr. Hatford, before you rewrite it as a scene.

- Remember that scenes are little stories within stories. Each scene has a high point somewhere in it. It may not be very exciting, but it's a little more exciting than the other parts of the scene.

SECTIONS
Explanation

A *section* in nonfiction is just like a scene in fiction, but instead of showing a reader a small piece of the plot, the section takes a simple idea and shows it to the reader with examples, anecdotes, description, and narrative. Here's an example from an essay in *The Lives of a Cell* by Lewis Thomas. The simple idea is that "ant colonies act like people."

EXAMPLE

> Ants are so much like human beings as to be an embarrassment. They farm fungi, raise aphids as livestock, launch armies into wars, use chemical sprays to alarm and confuse enemies, capture slaves. The families of weaver ants engage in child labor, holding their larvae like shuttles to spin out the thread that sews the leaves together for their fungus gardens. They exchange information ceaselessly. They do everything but watch television.

Thomas doesn't just *tell* us that ants are like people. He *shows* us five different things ants do that human civilizations have also done: farming, raising livestock, employing slavery and child labor, and exchanging information.

A nonfiction section doesn't just show examples, it has a pattern or a plan. The ant examples are presented in the order of the growth of human civilization, from farming to television.

Do you think Thomas organized his section on the first draft? Probably not. More likely, he first wrote down six ways ants act like people in his first draft. Then he decided to organize those six ways by the order of the rise of human civilizations. He might have had to find out whether farming or herding came first. He might have had to throw out an example that didn't fit the plan. Then he rewrote the whole thing. This is how writing nonfiction often works.

Writing a nonfiction section is a lot like cleaning out a closet. First, you must take out all the junk. (You call it *research*, but it is really just a bunch of ideas, examples, facts, descriptions and so forth — junk until you do something with it.) Once you've piled everything up, you decide which particular junk you want to put in this particular closet and get rid of the junk you don't want. *Then* you put everything away in the closet following a plan. It looks wonderful once you've finished, but getting it done is messy.

Because writing nonfiction is always messy, it is a good idea to plan on writing three trial drafts:

First trial— choose your simple idea and get the interesting details down.

Second trial— organize it into a little plan or pattern:
- throw out details that don't fit
- organize those you save
- add more details if necessary

Third trial— rewrite it in order to tidy everything up and smooth it out.

The nonfiction writer writes each section weaving together examples, anecdotes, description, and narrative, much like the fiction writer weaves dialogue and action together to make a scene. But the nonfiction writer does not use quite so many different tools; normally, nonfiction writers combine narrative with one other tool. Thomas uses only examples and one narrative sentence: "Ants are so much like people as to be an embarassment."

All of the fiction tools are also used in nonfiction. Sections of some types of nonfiction, such as personal experience stories, are written like fiction scenes, but you won't find much dialogue, action, or introspection in other types of nonfiction:

Example: a specific instance of something

Anecdote: a thumbnail story illustrating a point

Description: describes people, places, or things

Narrative: as in fiction, narrative tells the story, explains the point, or gives reasons

See specific explanations in this chapter for more detail on each of these.

Tricks of the Trade

- Information makes nonfiction interesting. Notice how much information about ant behavior Thomas packs into one small paragraph. If you are having trouble with a nonfiction section, go get more information. Read more books; look up more facts; make yourself into an expert. The better you know your subject, the easier it is to write nonfiction.

TRANSITIONS
Explanation

Transitions are those parts of the writing that concern moving from one chapter to the next, from one scene or section to the next, from one paragraph to the next, from one sentence to the next. Think of a transition as a little bridge that carries your reader from one part of the writing to another. Transitions themselves can vary in length. A transition can be a paragraph, a sentence, or just a word or two that leads the reader on. Remember Hooks and Leaders in chapter 3? The leader is really just a transitional sentence leading from the hook into the main body of the piece.

Transitions are one of the most difficult parts of writing both fiction and nonfiction. Not only do you need to make the move, you need to make it clearly so that you do not lose the reader in the process, and you want to make it unobtrusively with as few words as possible. There are as many ways to make transitions as there are writers. Below are four useful methods. (Note: In order to save space, we use ... to indicate places where the story goes on for several paragraphs or pages. You can fill in the gap with your imagination.)

1. Repeat a key term both before and after the move.

   EXAMPLE: A transition between two paragraphs using the key term *polar bear*

   People have for many years been fascinated by the *polar bear*, but now scientists are most interested in their survival.
   Polar Bears [transition] require large territories, give birth to few young, and do not mix well with civilization...

   Instead of repeating the key term, you can use a similar word or phrase, such as "this magnificent animal" or "the white bear of the Arctic."

2. Another method of making a transition is to set up a transition before making it. The set-up can come much earlier in the piece or just before the transition.

   EXAMPLE (nonfiction: changing to a new section)

   James Madison kept notes of the constitutional convention, *contributing to our present understanding of the constitution as much as the document itself...*
   Madison's notes [transition] are the most complete minutes of the convention. The official secretary found keeping track of the debates too difficult, and the convention was closed to the press.

   EXAMPLE (fiction: changing the scene)

   Jenny almost forgot that *she had promised to meet Peter at the airport that evening...*
   The airport was chaos [transition]. It seemed that half the city was either coming or going.

3. A third transition method is the break. This is much like a cut to another scene in a movie. The break is indicated by four blank lines, a subtitle, or the double pound sign (##).

EXAMPLE (cutting to a new scene with a new character)

Susan went to bed and lay in the dark, puzzled by Pattie's bitter words.

# #

Bill watched the sweaty cab driver slowly count his fare. No one trusts other people any more, he thought.

The break must be a sharp change of scene or time. Writers often use the other transitional techniques in addition to the break to make sure the reader understands the change.

4. There are many words that help writers make transitions. They can be used anywhere in the transitional sentence, but they are usually used as soon as possible. Below is a starter list.

TRANSITIONAL WORDS AND PHRASES

Transitions in Time

when	that morning (afternoon, evening)
the next day	on Monday
before	after
once	by the time
afterward	after that
next	still
while	in the meantime
at the time	many years (months) later
as long as	throughout
until	for (*for the next five years*)
over (*over five years*)	during
all through	the first time ... the next time
all the time	up to this point
just as	the first time (the last time)
later	recently (currently)
as yet	This wasn't the first time ... once before

Transitions of place

At the [place]

In [place]

Foreshadow the change of place by having a character anticipate going there. (E.g., "John knew Trenton was a rough town. He had never been there and wasn't looking forward to it ... *The streets of Trenton* [transition] were covered with wet litter. John walked down one alley.") Remember that a change of place usually involves some change of time as well, so time changes can be used for both.

Contrasting Ideas or Descriptions

however	by contrast
nonetheless (nevertheless)	despite
but (yet)	normally (usually)
even though	although
either ... or	neither ... nor

on the one hand ... on the other hand

on the one side ... on the other

in that case ... but in this case

_____believe that ... _____believe that

Ironically, (happily, tragically, or other introductory phrases)

Supporting Ideas or Descriptions

according to	one of the
even worse	worse yet
even better	better yet
for example	such as
what's more	one of the
in addition to	finally

first ... second ... third

in the first place ... furthermore ... moreover

more important than _____ is (was) _____.

numbering paragraphs or lists

Wrapping Up

therefore	thus
in conclusion	as a result
for these reasons	owing to
in summary (to summarize)	ultimately

Some of these transitional words can become a crutch for the lazy writer. If your work is loaded with *moreovers*, *therefores*, and *thuses*, try making transitions by the first method, repeating key words, until you break the habit.

Tricks of the Trade

- If your rough draft of a piece seems confusing or poorly organized, double check your transitions before doing anything else. Clumsy or confusing transitions can make pieces that are well organized seem disorganized.

- It is easy to fall into the habit of using the same transition method for every piece even though another method might work better. Try writing transitions using several different methods until you feel comfortable with a variety of methods. The better you get at using a variety of transitions, the easier writing will become.

Chapter 5

Editing with Enthusiasm

An editor should tell the writer his work is better than it is; not a lot better, a little better.

—T. S. Eliot

INTRODUCTION

Editing is an acquired taste, right up there with oysters and fried squid. Once you learn to edit, however, you may become addicted. After all, the perfect first draft is an awful burden. It kills creativity with premature judgment and makes drafting harder by mixing the artist and the craftsman.

Editing is the writer's secret weapon. The dancer, the golfer, and the pianist have one chance. They can't go back and cut out mistakes or splice a little improvement into a sloppy performance. The writer can. In a way, the writer must. Unlike singers, writers rarely produce a perfect performance on the first draft; each new piece is a new creation, improvised from scratch. Writers reach their peak through editing.

Despite the practical value of editing, few beginning writers do much of it. If they do edit, they content themselves with checking the spelling and a little minor polishing—not serious editing in the eyes of a professional. Beginners tend to view editing as simply mechanically correcting mistakes, but experienced writers treat editing as a vital part of the creative process. When you first begin to create something—a painting, a piece of furniture, or a piece of writing—you start with a mental picture of how you want it to turn out. Few people achieve that vision on the first try. In fact, few pieces end up exactly as one first imagines. Nevertheless, adjusting the initial draft to more closely match those expectations is as vital to creating the piece as the first draft. Only when the scramble to put ideas on paper is over can you finally see a physical creation instead of a fuzzy idea. Only then can you slow down, look at the work objectively, and adjust it bit by bit until you feel satisfied.

Beginners may need to edit more than experienced writers. For one thing, editing teaches you more about writing than any other part of the writing process. Each time you revise a piece until you feel a solid internal thud of satisfaction, you learn a little more. You may not be able to explain what you have learned, but you always learn something. For another thing, many beginning writers discover the joy of writing only when they edit a draft over and over until they feel confident that this is their best—and it's pretty darned good.

Separating Revision and Polishing

There are two phases to editing: revision and polishing. Revision includes such items as improving clarity, structure, and readability. Polishing includes checking the sentences for style, grammar, usage (the meanings of words), punctuation, and spelling. Take a tip from us: Don't try to revise and polish simultaneously. *Finish* revising before you begin to polish. Skipping one phase or the other, mixing the two phases, or taking them in the wrong order invariably creates more work and causes problems.

When you first begin to seriously edit, put your muscle into revision. Revision means "to see again." The first thing you do when you revise is, of course, read your own work. You see it again, but with a difference. You want to see it like a reader seeing it for the first time. Ask yourself questions such as, "Is this clear?" Looking through the reader's eyes, try to find honest, specific answers, then revise until you think it is clear. Crystal clear. Try another question, "Is it easy to follow?" Read the work with fresh eyes studying the organization and then revise it again. You can go through many revisions. The point is to keep going until you achieve results that will satisfy both you and your reader.

For the writer, revision is the heart and soul of editing because revision is writing based. It starts from the same creative vision you used to draft. You can discuss changes with the same terms and the same ideas as those used for drafting. In short, you use what you know about writing for both drafting and revision. For some writers, writing *is* revision. Only then do they finally nail down what they want to say and how they want to say it.

Polishing, on the other hand, is not writing based. Each area of polishing grows out of skills almost entirely separate from the rest of writing. Even the terminology is different. For example, you don't need to know the difference between a subject and a verb to draft a good piece of action, but you may need to know the subject from the verb to punctuate that action. This means that a person can know the rules of punctuation backward and forward but still write slow, dull action. Bad writing. The reverse is also true. Many talented writers cheerfully admit that their punctuation is shaky, even though they write well and publish often.

This is a confusing point, so be careful. Of course, punctuation and spelling are connected with writing. If you don't know the rules of punctuation, you may try to write only sentences that you know how to punctuate instead of writing what you really want to say. A bad idea. Similarly, you may be tempted to use a word that you know how to spell rather than the right word. Another bad move. When you do this, you let polishing problems spoil your writing. Save the polishing problems for polishing. By all means, learn the rules of punctuation, but learn them separately from writing and editing. You will improve your writing as well as the polish of your work.

Polishing the physical appearance of a piece is the last step to polishing and worth special mention. Polishing the presentation can include anything from making a neat handwritten copy to a full-scale printing. It does not have anything to do with writing per se. A messy but well written story is still well written. On the other hand, the world may permit F. Scott Fitzgerald to send in manuscripts scribbled on the backs of envelopes. It is less tolerant of the rest of us. An attractive presentation can be the difference between a sale and a rejection slip for the professional writer. Student writers rarely get full credit for good writing if the presentation is a mess.

You can treat presentation as one step in the polishing precess or as a separate phase of editing. The important thing is leaving plenty of time for it. Retyping or even fiddling with the printer on a word processor takes more time than writers like to admit. But it is the only way to make your work look as good as it is.

Distinguishing Editing from Criticism

Criticism can be devastating to writers. T. S. Eliot moved to England and could not write for a year and a half after a heavy bout with some critics. It damages all writers, but especially beginners, to throw their hearts into writing something if they don't also protect themselves from the fickle opinions of critics.

Writers who are editing do need a friendly ear, a fresh pair of eyes, and a different point of view to help them find places that need improvement. They also need a sharp mind to suggest possible changes. Finally, they need a pat on the back to boost their flagging energy. The person who provides all these things is the editor. Good writers love good editors because they are the writer's biggest help and best friends.

Before you can edit either your own work or other people's successfully, you must distinguish editing from criticism. People can be surprisingly cruel about writing as you may have discovered. Don't let a few bad experiences with criticism scare you away from editing, however. The job of the editor and that of the critic only appear similar. There are big differences—differences often overlooked.

Editors edit. They don't jump in while the writer is still drafting, and they don't bother commenting after it is too late to make changes. Anyone who jumps in too soon or too late is a critic, not an editor.

No sane writer shares a rough draft in order to be shot to pieces—even if those holding the guns claim to be helping. Editors spend as much time pointing out what is good about a piece as they do bird-dogging problems. Critics concentrate on criticism. This makes all the difference to the writer. When writers begin to edit, they are *still* writing and have a long way to go. They are already tired and need encouragement to carry on, or they will never finish. Helping the writer finish is the editor's number one goal, so working with a conscientious editor is as exciting to the writer as listening to a thoughtless critic is tedious.

Once a piece is finished, anybody has a right to comment. These are critics. They can say whatever they please. Some critics are serious; others are just showing off at the expense of the writer; some are thoughtful; some just silly. You should always consider the comments of a helpful editor, but you have every right to ignore a critic. You did not ask for the critic's opinion, and you do not need to listen—even if the critic is a teacher or a hot-shot novelist.

You do not need to listen even if the critic is yourself. Face it. Sometimes, we are our own worst critics. When you attack your own writing, always ask yourself, "Is this comment going to help me write a better piece or learn something new for the next piece?" If it doesn't help you do one or the other, forget it. Breast-beating just wastes time better spent writing.

INTRODUCTION TO EDITING

Let's be honest. The best way to learn to edit is to follow a good example. In the perfect world each beginning writer would take several manuscripts all the way through the editing process under the guidance of a skilled editor. So much for pipe dreams. Editing is one of the last great crafts in an age of mass production. It takes so long to train editors that, these days, skilled editors are about as rare as large diamonds. Most people never meet a top-notch editor. You must make the best of teachers, friends, and fellow writers. Most of all, you must teach yourself to be a competent editor, so you can edit your own work well.

This section's springboards will help you start. The first springboard reviews the editorial process and lays out a few basic rules. The second helps you learn to edit with other people, and the third is one of the best ways we have found to analyze your work and decide what to change.

Springboard 1: The Editing Process

Few processes are more wonderful ... than that of making your manuscript shine where it was rusty, tighten where it was flabby, speak clearly where it mumbled. —Paul Darcy Boles

Writing a story or an article is a little like creating a garden. The work doesn't end with planting and watering. The gardener has weeds to pull, dead plants to remove, and new plants to add before the garden looks its best. So does the writer. There are weedy words to pull, unclear sentences to straighten out, sections that need to be rearranged—all to make the writing its shining best.

Both editing and garden cleanup can get messy, particularly in the middle stages. You may know what you want, but the bystander just sees marginal scribbles and chopped up paragraphs. At times, you will wonder if you can ever put all the pieces back together. It is surprisingly easy to get lost in the mess. That's why it is very important to follow an editing process. When you use a process, at least you know which steps you've done and where you are, even though you can't yet see the results.

You can set up any editing process that works for you. The following diagram lays out the usual steps in simplified form:

	(cooling period)		*(cooling period)*		*(cooling period)*	
DRAFTING	VISION		REVISION	POLISHING		
	1. clean copy		1. analysis	1. style		
	2. review prewriting choices & outline		2. cut	2. mechanics		
			add	3. presentation		
	3. priority goal		rearrange			
			rewrite			

Cooling Periods. When you edit your work, your attitude is very important. Remember the artist and the craftsman? (See chapter 3.) Well, the artist is in charge of drafting, but the craftsman is in charge of editing. The artist is enthusiastic, emotional, involved, and sensitive. The craftsman, on the other hand, is more like Spock in *Star Trek.* Spock is concerned, but detached and logical. While everyone else runs around yelling, Spock stays cool. He listens and comes up with ideas to solve the problem. He's also patient and takes things one step at a time.

Because the attitude of the craftsman is almost the opposite of the artist, you must find a way to tell your artist to take a vacation before you can edit. This is very hard to do. For most people, the only way to make the change is through a cooling period. How much cooling works depends on the person. Twenty-four hours is usually the minimum. One cooling period between each phase seems to work best for most people.

Vision. As you draft, one thing leads to another. You tend to grow further and further away from your original vision of the piece. Before you edit, you need to study where you stand and to compare it to your original ideas. The first thing you need is a good, clean copy of the draft. Trying to see what you have through scribbles and marginalia is difficult. When you recopy the draft, leave double or triple spacing in order to have plenty of space for editing. Write on one side of the page, so that you can cut and paste with scissors and tape. (If you are using a word processor, this is a good time to put the draft on the machine.)

Next, update your prewriting choices checklist and your planning outline. You don't necessarily need to bring the draft in line with your planning. You may have come up with a better idea while you drafted. You do need to review where you ended up and think about whether or not that is what you want.

Finally, read quickly through the draft and try to set one general goal for editing. "Reduce wordiness" or "structure more clearly" are sufficient. Don't choose more than one goal: you need one top editing priority. Once you have a clear vision of where you stand and where you want to go, you are ready to start revising.

Revision. You want to make sure your piece is easy to understand and fun to read first. Revision is always exciting because you can shape what you said to sound just like you wish without worrying about deciding what to say, as you did when you drafted the piece. Generally, revision is easier if you do some analysis—deciding what to change and why—before you tackle cutting, adding, rearranging and revising. As you do more revising, you will find that you may actually become too brutal, rather than too tender. You can edit the life out of a piece, so try to stay balanced, changing only those things that need it.

Polishing. Polishing puts the final gloss on your work. When you polish, you first work on the style of the sentences. Next, you tackle the mechanics: grammar, punctuation, usage, and spelling. You also change any little thing that you feel would smooth out the writing. The last step of polishing is typing or neatly recopying the piece so that your presentation is attractive and easy to read.

You don't need to take a complete piece all the way through the process at once. You can edit one chapter at a time or one section at a time. Suit your own tastes. At some point, of course, you will need to edit the whole piece. But for some people, that final overall editing is easier if all the pieces are more or less finished. We only recommend that you use some kind of process and separate revision and polishing.

Try It

Choose a short piece from your practice journal to take all the way through the editing process. Try to choose a piece without strings attached: deadlines and expectations. It is easier to learn to edit when you feel you can do anything necessary, irrespective of the time it takes. It is also easier when you edit to satisfy your own expectations rather than someone else's.

We're going to discuss revision and polishing in more detail later, but in the meantime, we have some rules that apply to all the phases of the editing process. We call them the Golden Rules of Editing.

THE GOLDEN RULES OF EDITING (FILESHEET)

Rule #1: When in doubt, read out loud.

The most important part of editing is reading the work out loud to be sure that it sounds just like the author wants it to sound. If you have a question, read the whole piece, the paragraph, or the sentence out loud. Does it sound right? If it sounds right, it probably is.

Rule #2: Take your time.

Editing takes time, but it is time well spent because editing takes your good work and makes it the best it can be. If you are tired, wait a little before starting back to work. Editing at a steady pace with small breaks always works better than a crash project.

Rule #3: Don't mix revision and polishing.

Finish revising before you start to polish. Mixing revision and polishing always makes a mess. Also, finish each step of the polishing before you begin the next. Editing is always easier if you work on one thing at a time.

Rule #4: Always work from big to little.

Start with big changes, such as moving whole sections or scenes around. Work back to little things, such as changing a word in a sentence. It makes no sense to revise a sentence if you cut it out five minutes later when you move a whole section around.

Rule #5: Finish.

If you don't finish, how well you write or the care you take to polish won't matter a bit. Nobody can read it until it's done. You can take little pauses to refresh your energy, but otherwise just do the best job you can and keep going until you finish.

Springboard 2: The Editor? Who's That?

No passion in the world is equal to the passion to alter someone else's draft.
— H. G. Wells

You must draft alone, but you don't need to edit alone. You can get help from someone else's craftsman—an editor. The editor can be a fellow student, a friend, or a teacher. Better yet, you can work with several editors by forming an editorial group. You don't need to go far. There are people all around you who are writing and also need editors. All you need to do is find three our four who are willing to meet regularly to edit one another's work.

Because reading a rough draft to strangers is a frightening, unpredictable process, we suggest that you plan to keep the group together for at least a year. You can add people to the group, but do it gradually. If the group gets larger than about eight, split into two groups. The more you work together, the better you will get.

When the group meets, sometimes you will be an author and sometimes you will be an editor for another member of the group. This works well, as long as both authors and editors all remember that both are really craftsmen working together. We don't want to be negative, but we must warn you that when either authors or editors do not act like calm, detached craftsmen, the group will have trouble.

When authors act like artists

- they won't listen
- they argue over everything
- they get upset
- they take every comment as a criticism
- they tire out and don't want to finish
- they are impatient

When editors are bad craftsmen

- they criticize without helping
- they don't take their jobs seriously
- they make fun of the author or show off at the author's expense
- they aren't specific
- they don't make helpful suggestions

If the members of your writing group work together as craftsmen, you'll be dynamite. You can help each other so much that you won't believe it. To get your group off to a good start, we've included a filesheet, the Editorial Group Pledge. If your group follows these principles, you will look back on forming the group as the best thing you ever did for your writing.

Try It

Pass this out when you form the group or add new people. Enforce your pledges. Incidentally, some editorial groups like to give the group a name. It seems to help the group establish an identity and hold together. Try it!

Good Editors

1. Good editors are good craftsmen. They learn as much as they can about writing and apply what they know in a detailed, careful way.

2. Good editors are specific. They don't say, "That's dumb," or "I like that." They say, "Your high point needs more suspense," or "The description in this scene is really good."

3. Good editors don't boss. It's the author's piece, not the editor's. The good editor makes good suggestions and leaves decisions to the author.

4. Good editors help the author finish. They give the author some pats on the back and say, "Keep going. You're almost finished, and I know you can do it."

5. Good editors help the author take things one step at a time until it's done.

6. Good editors take the job seriously. They feel as proud of the finished piece as the author. And well they should.

Professional Authors

1. Professional authors come prepared. They bring clean copies of their drafts for each editor. They review plans and outlines, leave a cooling period between drafting and editing, and choose a primary goal before they come to the group.

2. Professional authors don't argue. They ask questions to draw out the editors and they take notes. They make final decisions on their own.

3. Professional authors don't waste editorial time. They only bring pieces on which they want comments, and they do everything possible to focus precious editorial time on important questions.

4. Professional authors let editors know when comments are especially helpful so that everyone learns.

5. Professional authors take their writing seriously and try to give each piece their very best.

THE EDITORIAL GROUP PLEDGE (FILESHEET)

The members of this group agree to the following pledges:

1. We will meet regularly and start on time. We will only work on editing and save social conversation for other times.

2. We will be honest with one another, knowing that we don't want compliments or criticism: we want help.

3. At all times, we will approach editing like good editors and professional authors.

Springboard 3: The Revision Loop

What is true of friendship is true of editing; ... I have tried to remember that it was my job to help when the author needed it, to reassure him, to call out of him his best, but always to bear in mind that the final decision was his.

—Edward Weeks

For some people the first draft holds no thrills; they only begin to write seriously when they begin to revise. Their motto is, "Just give me a telephone directory, anything but a blank page. I'll revise it into something." In every group of people who write, a few catch fire once they discover revision.

A reader may think that a piece turned out perfectly the first time, but the writer knows better. Good writers revise and revise and revise until they are satisfied that their work sounds just right. Did you know that Ernest Hemingway revised the end of *A Farewell to Arms* thirty-nine times? Most professionals revise every piece at least four or five times. That's why their writing sounds so good.

There are few good books on revision. What you do depends on what you wrote, so the best way to learn to revise is by revising. There is, however, one good book that will give you plenty of ideas on what types of things to revise, and that is Theodore Cheney's *Getting the Words Right: How to Revise, Edit, and Rewrite*. Every page has interesting ideas you can apply somewhere in your own work.

Of course, you don't need to revise everything thirty-nine times, but you should learn to revise your work until you are satisfied that it sounds right. "The Revision Loop" is a simple, positive procedure to follow in order to identify portions of the draft that need revision and decide how to change them. If you are using the loop with your editing group, make sure that the members of the group already feel comfortable sharing their work with the group. Before you use the loop, practice reading aloud to the editing group just identifying the best part, not getting into other comments.

THE REVISION LOOP (FILESHEET)

1) Group chooses an editorial question

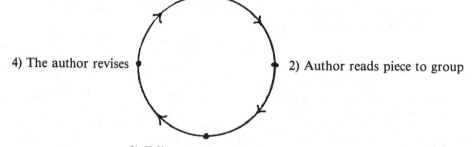

4) The author revises

2) Author reads piece to group

3) Editors make editorial suggestions

STEP 1. The group starts around the loop by choosing an editorial question.

Editorial questions can be about almost anything: "What is the best part?" "How can the author make the dialogue fit the characters better?" "Which sections are not clear?" "How can the author make the end more satisfying?" "How should the author add suspense?" (See "Basic Editorial Questions Filesheet," p. 138, for ideas on questions to ask.)

Choosing those editorial questions which will most help the author is the trick to revising. You can go around the loop as many times as you wish, but there are a thousand possible editorial questions. Editors and authors should go around on at least the three or four questions that they think will most help the author.

The group can choose any questions they wish except for the first question. The first editorial question is always "What is the best part?" Strangely, authors do not know which parts of their own stories are best. If their editors forget to mention which parts are best, the authors may accidentally throw them out when they revise.

STEP 2. One of the editors reads the piece aloud while the author and other editors listen carefully, keeping the editorial question in mind.

Reading aloud is the most important part of editing. Revision may be a bad choice of word because authors and editors do not need to *see* a piece; they need to *hear* it. Remember, writing is like singing. Until a piece is read aloud, it is like an unsung song. It is a good idea to have someone besides the author read because the author will smooth over problems that another person might stumble on, and those are just the places that you are trying to locate. If you run across a real klunker—a confusing typo or a totally scrambled sentence—just correct it quickly, so the group doesn't waste time on it, but, otherwise, the group should not concern itself with polishing errors yet.

STEP 3. The editors make editorial suggestions.

Suppose the editors decide to tell the author that the high point needs more suspense. Do they say, "Make the high point more suspenseful"? No. They say, "I think your high point needs more suspense. Remember that paragraph right before the train moved through the tunnel—the one where the children were walking along the train tracks? Maybe you could stretch that out just a little longer and make us worry a little more about what will happen when the train comes through the tunnel." They don't say, "Unclear." They say, "I didn't quite understand the paragraph where you explain how organic chemistry ties into Chinese history. Could you give an example?"

When you are an editor, remember that you really need to think hard about your suggestions. Be specific. Give the author your best ideas, then let the author decide what to do.

STEP 4. The author looks at the editors' suggestions, decides what to do, and makes the revisions.

In the last step on the loop the author makes changes to the piece. The group can wait for the author to make the changes before going around the loop with another editorial questions or the group can go around the loop several times before the author revises.

Try following these rules when revising your work: Always work from big to little. Work on whole sections first, paragraphs next, then sentences, and finally individual words. When you revise, you can cut, rearrange, add, or rewrite. Try doing them in this order:

1. *Cut first.* When you cut out unnecessary sections, paragraphs, sentences, or words, you clear away everything which might cover up the good parts of your story. It's just like a gardener pulling weeds and trimming away dead branches in order to show off the pretty flowers.

2. *Rearrange second.* Once you have the weeds cleared out, you can see your story better. You can rearrange the order of the paragraphs into a clearer design. Use a pair of scissors and a roll of tape to cut the draft apart and rearrange the order.

3. *Add third.* Add any improvements you think would help your newly rearranged draft.

4. *Rewrite last.* Rewrite any sentences or paragraphs that you think need it. Sometimes it is easier to rewrite a sentence or a paragraph than to try to fix it. Rewriting last usually saves time.

BASIC EDITORIAL QUESTIONS (FILESHEET)

To help editors think of specific ideas, these editorial questions are arranged with a basic editorial question followed by follow-up questions that are more specific. Of course, this is just a starter list. Add questions that interest you to your own list.

Nonfiction

1. What is the best part? Why?

2. Does the piece suit the ideal reader? Is the information appropriate to that ideal reader? Is there anything missing that the ideal reader would probably like to learn?

3. How does the mood add to the piece? Did the author maintain the same mood all the way through? Are there any sections where the mood is inconsistent?

4. Does the author say what he wants to say? What is the key idea? Does that key idea come across loud and clear?

5. What is the most interesting piece of information in the piece? How was it presented? Was it presented in the right place?

6. Did the writer use examples or anecdotes? Did they make the piece more fun to read? Could the piece use more examples or another anecdote?

7. Where is the piece easiest to understand? Are there any places where the piece is hard to understand? Why? What could the author do to make it clearer?

8. Are there any unnecessary parts of the piece? Why aren't they necessary? Could the author cut it? How would cutting it improve the piece?

9. Choose two of the following words to describe the piece and explain why you chose it.

crisp	informative	funny	relaxed
serious	compact	detailed	helpful
organized	well-researched	entertaining	fresh ideas
clear	flowing	sparkling	musical

10. If you could suggest one change that the author make, what would it be? Why?

Fiction

1. What is the best part? Why?

2. Are the characters easy to picture? What makes each important character interesting? Are the things they do consistent with their personalities? Does the dialogue fit the characters?

3. Who is the most interesting character? Why?

4. Which scene turned out best? Why?

5. Was the story easy to follow? Was there anything that did not make sense? Why?

6. Is the story even? Were some scenes cut too short or others a bit too long? What could the author do to even the story out?

7. Was the ending satisfying? Did the author tie up all the loose ends or, for example, did you end up wondering what happened to some characters? What could the author do to tie up loose ends and/or make the ending more satisfying?

8. Where is the best action, description, dialogue, or introspection in the story? Are there any places where the story could use more of any of these?

9. Are there any unnecessary scenes, characters, or other parts of the story? Why aren't they necessary? How would cutting them improve the story?

10. Does the crisis or high point have enough suspense to hold the reader? If not, what could the author do to add a little more suspense?

11. Choose two of the following words to describe the piece and explain why you chose those two.

snappy	moody	action-packed	suspenseful
relaxed	thoughtful	sparkling	musical
flowing	intriguing	well-plotted	inspiring
entertaining	funny	well-researched	serious

12. If you could suggest one change that the author make, what would it be?

Notes from the Pros:
On Managing the Editing Time

Planning and drafting is slow work, but editing is glacial. If you allow twice as much time for editing as drafting, you won't be far off the mark. Writing is a slow-paced business in a fast-paced world. Even when you discover the joy of editing, time management can prove to be a headache. Delays in planning and drafting pile up on editing, and editing seems to proceed at its own snail-like pace. It will not be pushed. If your editing often suffers from deadline pressure, here are a few hints to help you cope:

- Set personal deadlines well ahead of the actual deadlines. If that paper is due on September 30, plan to finish by September 25. There are just too many unanticipated problems that can pop up leaving you to edit in a panic.

- Set one deadline between revision and polishing, another between polishing and final presentation. Both revision and polishing can go on endlessly. Sometimes you just have to call an arbitrary halt to it. You should not skip any one phase of editing, so it's best to allot time for each in advance.

- Know your priorities. You may not have time to take every writing assignment through a full-scale revision and polishing. Don't skip revision or polishing, just cut each one back a little. Your time is still best spent revising. After all, you are the only one who can revise your own work. Someone else can check the spelling or retype it for you if time runs short.

- Get help. It may take you hours to spot an error that a friend will find in thirty seconds. If you don't have an editorial group, form one. An editorial group will not only help you edit more easily, it will help you edit faster.

- Use a word processor. Word processors were designed to speed up revision and polishing. (Incidentally, you don't need to draft on a word processor; just type up your rough draft before you edit.) Word processors make adding and cutting material so easy that you will be more inclined to edit and do a better job. Nothing encourages editing like knowing that the exhausting retyping job ahead is for practical purposes already done.

    If you don't own a word processor, you can probably find a place on campus that rents them to students for a nominal fee. Be aware of a couple of problems, however, First of all, word processors only save time once you know how to use them. If you wait until the last minute to learn how to use a particular word processing program, you will probably find yourself fighting with the print command at midnight the day before the deadline. Learn the program in advance. Secondly, although most word processors these days have spelling checkers and so-called style checkers, they are very crude tools. The spelling checker will miss a lot of misspellings, and the style checkers pick up only fairly obvious errors in grammar and punctuation. Don't rely on them too heavily. No computer can substitute for your intelligence and good judgment.

- Write without deadlines occasionally. Constantly writing and editing against a deadline can wear you out. Besides, you may never be able to do all the revising and polishing required to produce your very best. When you work against a deadline, it's usually a case of doing the best you can in the time available, instead of doing the very best you are capable of doing. If you are tired of deadline pressures, take a break. Work on a piece that no one expects you to turn in. So what if it takes you a year to complete? It will be good for your psyche and very good for your writing.

Student's Notebook:
On Grades

Grades do everything that good editors should not. Good editors are specific; grades aren't. Good editors help writers finish; grades don't. Good editors don't act like critics; grades do. Grades teach students to measure their work against the opinion of just one person—something writers should never do. It is difficult to conceive of a worse editorial system than the traditional mark and grade. It converts teachers into critics even when they would rather be editors. Short of changing the system, there are a surprising number of things *you* can do to liberate the editors in your instructors.

Treat your teachers like good editors. When you treat people like good editors, they tend to rise to your expectations and respond like good editors. Many students never talk with their professors. It's hard for any good editor to work long distance. Most professors have office hours for students. Make an appointment. Remember, good editors need to read the work, your professors won't remember yours. You can save time by leaving a copy of your piece at their offices ahead of time with a note explaining that you have an appointment to discuss the piece. You may want to include a few good editorial questions with your note.

Be professional. You have every right to question a grade that you don't understand or don't think is fair. But if you go into any discussion of your work hysterical, hostile, or interested only in the grade, not in the work, what kind of editing do you think you will receive? Probably, "Sorry Charlie." You earned it with your unprofessional behavior. Bring the same professional attitude to editing sessions with your teachers that you bring to editing sesisons with your editorial group. Come prepared. Focus on specifics. Don't argue, and don't waste valuable editorial time. You will have much better results.

The biggest problem with grades, of course, is that they come too late. Only *you* can do something about this. Try making an appointment for editorial advice *before* you revise. (Come in early; not the day before it's due.)

If you can't see the instructor ahead of time, make an appointment anyway. Even though you have received a grade, you can always ask to rewrite the piece. Surprisingly few students ask for rewrites. Surprising, because many teachers will agree to a rewrite even though it means more work for them. Even more surprising because a careful rewrite often results in a better grade. If you don't want to rewrite, you can still go over any comments on your returned pieces and add to your dirty dozen list (see Springboard 6). Use your imagination to find ways both to dig more specific comments out of your instructor and to put those comments to use improving the present piece or preparing for the next.

Grades are not specific enough to serve as editing. Don't assume a C means that you are a poor writer. If you don't know why you received a particular grade, ask. There are a thousand possibilities; you can't guess. After all, you may simply have less experience writing about Chinese history than the other members of the class. Sure, the writing may need work as well. You won't know until you ask.

Keep in mind that most college instructors are not writing teachers or trained editors. They got where they are through knowing about Chinese history, business management, or geology. Most have enough experience to know good writing when they see it, and many write well themselves, but editing is not that easy. Your instructors can tell you where your history or geology went haywire, and tell you that the writing went haywire, too, but they may have trouble explaining specifically where and how the writing went wrong. Give them some help. Ask questions. Ask to see good examples. If they still can't explain, see someone with more editing experience. Don't ever base your opinion of how well you write on the views of just one person. If you think it's good, have a little faith in yourself. Hans Christian Andersen's classic *Fairy Tales* was turned down by every publisher in Copenhagen. He published it himself.

POLISHING FOR AN INVISIBLE MANUSCRIPT

The second stage of editing—polishing—includes checking the usage (the meanings of words), grammar, punctuation, spelling, and, finally, the physical appearance of the manuscript. Think of yourself as a skilled cabinetmaker fine-sanding and finishing a beautiful piece of furniture. These mechanical details are not important to the writing. A badly spelled piece can still be well written. On the other hand, mechanical errors have the same effect as a scratch on a fine piece of furniture: they draw attention away from the virtues of the piece and focus attention on its flaws. You should spend as much time as you possibly can trying to make the mechanics invisible. You have won the polishing battle when your reader, engrossed in what you have to say, does not notice your polishing.

Writing takes as much endurance as it does talent or skill, endurance built by writing consistently every day over a long period of time. Writing is no different in this respect from sports that demand physical endurance. When beginners reach the polishing stage, many start to run out of steam. It isn't that they don't know how to correct the error or that they don't care. They are just too tired to do it. If you want to do a careful job, break polishing into small stages and take a rest between stages. The fewer things you try to cover in one pass through the draft, and the more rested you are between passes, the better you will do.

If you tend to be a perfectionist, try to be realistic. No matter how hard you try, you will not catch everything. We are willing to bet a dollar that there are some polishing errors in this section. Murphy's Law being what it is, the punctuation error is probably in the punctuation section. That does not mean that you should not try to polish carefully and catch everything you see. We all learn from our mistakes; every mistake you find and correct provides one more opportunity to learn something new.

Many students believe that somehow experienced writers know everything. Experienced writers like to encourage that belief: it boosts their egos. The truth is that all experienced writers cheat. They own plenty of books on polishing, and consult them routinely. Start building your own polishing library. It will help you more than you now realize. By the time you leave school, these books should be as comfortable as an old shoe, using them something you take for granted. Someday you, too, may wish to pretend that you know everything.

We suggest the following books. If you can't find the exact book, look for one that covers similar topics. Don't forget to look in used book stores if your budget is tight.

A spelling dictionary: A small dictionary with spellings only, for example, *The New Century Vest-Pocket 50,000 Words.*

A misspeller's dictionary: A dictionary of commonly misspelled words organized by common misspellings.

A grammar guide: Always own something like the *Harbrace College Handbook*, which explains grammar terms, punctuation rules, and other mechanics in detail.

A usage guide: We like Phyllis Martin's *Word Watcher's Handbook: A Deletionary of the Most Abused and Misused Words.*

A punctuation guide: We like Margaret Enright Wye's blessedly short *The Complete Guide to Punctuation: A Quick-Reference Deskbook*. We also like Barron's *The Art of Styling Sentences: 20 Patterns for Success* by Marie Wadell et al. — although it is a better learning tool than a reference book.

A style guide: The most famous is Strunk and White's *The Elements of Style*, but there are many other good choices. Gary Provost's delightful *100 Ways to Improve Your Writing* contains an excellent collection of style tips. Finally, the most complete style manual around is the famous *Chicago Manual of Style* from the University of Chicago Press, a fascinating — if overwhelming — tour of the publishing process, from punctuation rules for writers who are preparing manuscripts to printer's typefaces. It should have a subtitle: "everything you ever wanted to know about editing and more." It's worth owning a copy, so that you have at least one authoritative, thorough guide to consult for tricky questions. Recently, some other presses, such as the *New York Times* press, have published their style manuals in paperback. They are a little less complete than the *Chicago Manual*, but cheaper and less daunting. Finally, for those of you most interested in legal, business, or technical writing, Jefferson Bates's *Writing with Precision* is a priceless style guide.

In this section we have two springboards to help you. The first covers points of style you may wish to revise. The second, Polishing for Pride, has four filesheets on various polishing subjects.

Polishing always takes more time than one wishes, and it is the least interesting part of writing, but, because polishing errors are so visible, they usually receive more critical weight than they deserve. Spelling or grammar errors can blunt the impact of hours of research, planning, and drafting. Try to look at it from your reader's perspective. Careful polishing makes reading a pleasure, and readers appreciate the courtesy.

Springboard 4: Polishing for Style

It is not intentionally mannered writing that adds up to style, or richly poetic paragraphs, or the frantic pursuit of novel prose rhythms. The writer's own style emerges when he makes no deliberate attempt to have any style at all.

—Lawrence Block

Everyone wants to write with style even though no one can tell you what good style is. We think good style starts with writing simply and naturally in one's own words. When you start to polish, you can dig out the style rules, tricks of the trade (see chapter 4), and any writers whose technique you admire to help you polish the style of your sentences.

Try It

Professional writers use some simple little tricks to perk up sentences. You can use them too. Follow these little tips, and your style—whatever that is—should improve.

STYLE TIPS (FILESHEET)

TIP #1:   Use the *active voice*, not the passive, most of the time.

Passive: The stories *were written by* the students.
Active: The students *wrote* stories.

Passive: The pen *was broken by* Sue.
Active: Sue *broke* the pen.

Passive: The experiment *was done by* the students in Group One.
Active: The students in Group One *did* the experiment.

TIP #2:   Replace abstract nouns with more concrete nouns.

Abstract: Beautiful *flowers* lined the path.
Specific: *Blue bachelor buttons and purple daisies* lined the path.

Abstract: A *dog* ran along the fence barking at *people*.
Specific: A *German Shepherd* ran along the fence barking at *joggers*.

Don't overdo it. Use your judgment.

TIP #3:   Use simple, specific verbs.

General:	She *was sitting* in the car.
More specific:	She *waited* in the car.
	She *sulked* in the car.
	She *slept* in the car.

General:	He *went across* the room.
More specific:	He *marched* to the cupboard.
	He *slipped* across to the window.
	He *danced* across the room.

TIP #4:   "As" is a difficult word, especially in fiction. When you have used "as" in the middle of a sentence, try breaking the sentence into two sentences and reversing them.

One sentence:	I don't want to do this anymore, thought Sue as she tied another bow on another bouquet.
Two sentences, reversed:	Sue tied another bow on another bouquet. I don't want to do this anymore, she thought.
One sentence:	Jo wondered what the weather would be like when she got off the plane tomorow as the thunder cracked outside and the first drops of the storm rattled on the window.
Two sentences, reversed:	The thunder cracked outside and the first drops of the storm rattled on the window. Jo wondered what the weather would be like when she got off the plane tomorrow.

TIP #5: Once is enough. If you've said something twice, cut out the weaker one.

Twice: John walked across the kitchen and yanked open the refrigerator door. As he opened the refrigerator, a mouse ran out from under it.

Once: John walked across the kitchen and yanked open the refrigerator door. A mouse ran out from under it.

Twice: Hannibal led his men across the Alps and onto the plains of northern Italy. As they crossed the Alps, they fought snow and blinding hail and talked of victory once they reached the warm plains.

Once: As Hannibal's men crossed the Alps, they fought snow and blinding hail and talked of a victory ahead on the warm plains of northern Italy.

TIP #6: Replace long, dull words and phrases with short punchy ones.

He demonstrated his happiness.

He smiled.

TIP #7: Cross out unnecessary adverbs. Look for every word ending in *ly* and ask yourself if you need it. If not, cross it out. "She shouted" or "it was awesome" are better than "she shouted loudly" and "it was totally awesome."

TIP #8: Take out useless clutter words if possible:

a little	very	really
sort of	too	mostly
kind of	pretty much	
rather	quite	

TIP #9: Vary your sentence length. Strings of sentences all the same length make dull reading. This is especially true if the sentences have the same structure. "Joe went to the store. Mary read her book. The afternoon dragged on." Well, that string is boring and may work to reinforce the reader's sensation of a boring afternoon. Most of the time, however, you aren't describing boring afternoons. Give your reader variety. A paragraph should have a rhythm to it. A flow. Sometimes it's slow; sometimes fast. Some sentences short. Some long. Learn more punctuation if your limited knowledge of the rules keeps you from using a variety of sentences.

TIP #10: *THE BIG RULE*. Read every sentence out loud. Does it say something? Does it make sense? Does it sound clear and simple? Does it fit the mood of the writing? If not, rewrite it.

Some Style Tips That Don't Work

BAD TIP #1: "Put commas where you take a breath." Singers spend years learning where and how to breathe. So do writers. Expert writers, who know the rules of punctuation and proper breathing, can use this rule. If *you* try it, you may end up sprinkling commas everywhere sounding like you have a bad cold. Learn the rules of punctuation and use as few commas as possible.

BAD TIP #2: "Don't repeat words." This is nonsense. Good writers repeat words all the time. If you change every repeated word to another, you'll sound like a sportscaster. By all means, don't pound your reader to death repeating words. But a little repetition for rhythm and emphasis is fine.

Springboard 5: Polishing for Pride

Word carpentry is like any other kind of carpentry. You must join your sentences smoothly.

—Anatole France

Few things destroy a writer's ego so quickly as watching anxiously while a friend flips through a manuscript and, before reading one sentence, points to a big, fat spelling error. "All this work, and he only notices the spelling," the bruised writer grumbles with some justification. Mechanical errors in grammar, usage, punctuation, and spelling are like bees at a picnic. No matter how splendid the weather or tasty the food, one irritating bee dropping in for a bite to eat can spoil the whole effect. Instead of remembering the gorgeous day, people recall, "the picnic with the bee." Mechanical errors can cause your reader to remember how well you spell, not what you say. For the sake of your own pride, do your very best to get rid of every mechanical error.

The key to polishing mechanics (called "copyediting" in publishing houses) is simple: *find someone to help you.* Like all writers, students, too, suffer from manuscript blindness. Once a writer has reread a manuscript a certain number of times, even obvious errors become invisible.* If you haven't formed an editing group, at least ask a friend. Your friends don't need to be whizzes at punctuation or spelling to copyedit your work. They make mistakes, too, but they are not likely to make the same mistakes as you. If you share copyediting chores with a friend, you will each learn twice as much as you otherwise would.

---

* Teachers suffer from a special version of manuscript blindness. They see so many misspellings and punctuation errors in student work that their own spelling and punctuation deteriorates. The worst copyeditor in the world may be an English instructor in the month of May.

The other key to copyediting is to keep learning and relearning the rules. There are plenty of usage and punctuation rules to go around. Too many. You can't learn them all in one big gulp, so keep after them one little rule at a time. Also, be sure to break copyediting into little parts making many passes through the manuscript. You just can't remember to check too many things at once. If necessary, check the manuscript one punctuation rule at a time. This is tedious, but it will get easier over time.

This springboard has three filesheets to help you learn the rules and copyedit your own work. They are just quick reminders, not complete courses. The first, "The Dirty Dozen," explains a dozen common errors that you may want to correct in your own work. The second, "The Parts of a Sentence," briefly reviews a few useful terms, and the third, "Practical Punctuation," reviews a few of the most useful punctuation rules. The fourth is on the "Personality of Punctuation," a fun way to think about the art of punctuation, as opposed to the rules of punctuation.

Try It

Read through the filesheets and keep them handy when you copyedit.

THE DIRTY DOZEN (FILESHEET)

No one can correct overnight every error he or she commonly makes in grammar, usage, punctuation, or style. You need a short list. Otherwise, almost any grammar or style book will defeat you with the sheer number of rules to remember. This filesheet has a dozen common errors for you to check when you polish your work—the dirty dozen. Since we believe that it is more important to be clear than to be profound, we have selected problems that most often defeat clarity.

Our dirty dozen may not be your dirty dozen. You will develop your own list over time. Don't ignore the red scribblings on your returned papers. Study them; record them; ask about them. Make sure you know what the error was and how to correct it. If it is an error that you make often, put it on your dirty dozen list. Keep checking it until you don't make that error much; then replace it with a new villain.

ERROR #1:   Incomplete sentences

This is not the most common error people make, but it is one of the worst. With some very minor exceptions, every complete sentence must have at least one independent clause. An independent clause is a clause that can stand alone. Like all clauses, it has both a subject and a predicate. Remember, finding a subject and a predicate does not guarantee that the sentence is complete. A dependent clause (since we last saw him, before the storm struck) is not a complete sentence. Even though it does have a subject and a predicate, it cannot stand alone.

Of course, writers sometimes use incomplete sentences on purpose in order to add rhythm, emphasis, or clarity. You can use incomplete sentences in your writing as long as you do it deliberately and the meaning is clear. Before you deliberately use an incomplete sentence, however, ask yourself if the incompletion will startle or confuse the reader. If the answer is yes, use a complete sentence instead. Avoid deliberate incomplete sentences beginning with the words *when, if, since, before, after, because,* or *that* because they almost always surprise and confuse readers.

Almost everyone writes an accidental incomplete sentence every now and then. If, however, you frequently write incomplete sentences by accident, you have a big problem. You probably don't know what a complete sentence is, and this will hold your writing back forever, no matter how good your ideas or brilliant your metaphors. Take steps to correct the problem immediately. Your best option is a good grammar course. It is easier to learn grammar with someone on the spot to help. If you cannot find a course, buy a good handbook, such as *The Harbrace College Handbook*, and work your way through the chapters on sentences. If that overwhelms you, ask an instructor or a friend to help you untangle your misunderstandings, so you can get your writing on track.

ERROR #2:   Habitual wordy phrases

Every word in every sentence should work and work hard. Extra words that don't pull their weight clutter up the piece and confuse the reader. You can almost always improve your writing by substituting short, clear words for habitual wordy phrases, even if it means rewriting the sentence.

Change:	*To:*
advance planning	planning
afford the opportunity	permit
along the lines of	like
as of this date	today, on (date)
ask the question	ask, question
at an early date	soon
at the present time	now
at this point in time	now
be that as it may	but, nevertheless
blame it on_____	blame_____
by means of	with, by
consensus of opinion	consensus
continue on	continue
cooperate together	cooperate
curiously enough	curiously
due to the fact that	because
equally as	equally
estimated at about	estimated at
finalize	finish, end, complete
for the purpose of	for
for the reason that	because
frame of reference	point of view, background
have got	must, should
he is a man who	(cut "a man who")
hereby, thereby	(cut)
in a number of cases (instances	some, sometimes, often
in connection with	of, in, on
in my opinion	I think, I believe (or cut)
in order to	to
in the case of	if
in view of	because (or cut)
join together	join
learning experience	experience
meaningful (experience, relationship)	(cut)

needless to say	(cut)
never before in the past	never before, never in the past
on the basis of	by, because
on the part of	for
owing to the fact that	because
personal friend	friend
personally, I think	I think
presently	now, soon
prior to	before
relatively	(cut)
the fact that	(cut)
the question as to whether	whether
the reason is because	because, the reason for
there is no doubt that	no doubt, doubtless
this is a subject that	this subject
utilize	use
with the result that	so that
with reference to	about, referring to (or cut)

ERROR #3:   Subject-pronoun disagreement

The average person does not say, "*He* put the tire jack in *her* trunk" meaning "*He* put the tire jack in *his* trunk." This error is called a subject-pronoun disagreement. Grammar books go on for pages about it, but you will have trouble with it only in the three cases below:

- *With singular pronouns* (another, anybody, everyone, anything, each, any_____, anyone, either, everybody, everyone, every one of, everything, many a _____, neither, nobody, somebody, someone, one, no one). Because these pronouns are singular, you must use the singular pronouns *his, her,* or *its,* not the plural pronoun *their.*
    Everybody wants to improve *his* writing. (correct)
    Everybody wants to improve *his or her* writing. (correct)
    Everybody wants to improve *her* writing. (correct)
    Everybody wants to improve *their* writing. (incorrect)
    This problem has crept into speech because using *his* to mean *his or her* sounds sexist, but using *her* to mean *his or her* may startle or confuse readers. On the other hand, using *his or her* sounds clumsy, especially if you do it often. So in speaking, people have begun to use the plural *their* to mean *his or her.* Some writers predict that within thirty years or so this may become the accepted practice. But it has not changed yet. Pronouns such as each and everybody are singular and require the singular *his, her,* or *his or her.*

In a similar vein sentences such as "A writer wants to improve their writing" or "The grocer puts apples on their shelf" are also wrong. *Writer* and *grocer* are singular, so the sentences should read "A writer wants to improve his writing" and "The grocer puts apples on his shelf." If you don't like this, switch to the plural: "Writers want to improve their writing" and "Grocers put apples on their shelves."

- *With words for groups* (class, gang, gathering, flock, group, gathering, assembly, and so forth). Although the group may be made up of several individuals, there is only one group, so the pronoun should be the singular. Furthermore, even if the group is made up of people, the group itself has no gender, so the correct pronoun is *its*.

  The *gaggle* of geese picked *its* way south.

  The *crowd* shouted *its* approval.

  The *seminar* of lawyers cleaned up *its* mess and left.

  That *class* of students loved reading *its* work.

- *With two people of the same gender.* Suppose you have two characters—Jim and Bill—in a scene, and each man has a car. When you write, "Jim put the tire jack back in his trunk," whose trunk do you mean? Jim's or Bill's? You must study the sentence in context to be sure your reader understands. If it isn't clear, you may need to change to "Jim put the tire jack back in his own trunk."

ERROR #4: *They're, their, there, it's,* and *its*

Beware of these words, which sound the same in conversation but are written differently because of their grammatical and semantic differences. Double-check. Mistakes are easily made in the heat of drafting, and many college instructors list this as perhaps the most common error they see in student work.

- *They're* is a contraction meaning "they are." (*They're* coming tomorrow. *They're* not the ones you wanted.)

- *Their* is the plural possessive pronoun meaning "belonging to them." (They love to read *their* writing aloud. The mittens are *theirs*.)

- *There* describes a place or a state of being. (Put 'er *there* pardner. It's over *there*. *There* are three of them.)

- *It's* is a contraction meaning "it is." (*It's* not the one you wanted. *It's* high time you put in an apostrophe.)

- *Its* is the possessive pronoun meaning "belonging to it." (The dog played with *its* ball. The gang ran to *its* hideout.)

ERROR #5: *Not un-*

Change "He looked not unlike a troll" to "He looked like a troll."

Change "The champions were not unhappy with their game plan" to "The champions were happy with their game plan."

There is nothing grammatically wrong with the *not un-* construction, but it can enrage readers. The *not un-* leads them to believe that they are going to hear some small but vital distinction—and then leaves them hanging. What do you mean "not unlike a troll?" Was the guy a troll or not? Was he like a troll at all? Forty percent like a troll? How so? In what ways was he not like a troll? Oh, trolls don't have feathers and beaks like he did. Well, why didn't you say so?

If you use the *not un-* construction, be sure to give your reader some clue why you said "not unlike" or "not unhappy," instead of "like" or "happy." And you had better have a good reason. Otherwise, it's like giving trivial information in a conspiratorial whisper: readers feel cheated when they wait with bated breath to hear what turns out to be as commonplace as a recipe for hamburgers.

Warning: Once you start, the *not un-* habit can be as hard to break as smoking. Better never to start. Don't be too surprised to find a few *not un-*addicts among your professors. It plagues academic writing more than other kinds of writing.

ERROR #6: Too many *nots*

While we're on the subject of the word *not*, you are well-advised to scrutinize any sentence with the word *not* in it. Readers dislike the word. Too many *not*s grate on the nerves. Besides, when you use *not*, you may also lose the chance to use a more precise, livelier word. Try to write in positive statements, even when the thought is a negative one.

> He was not a good student.
> He was a poor student.
>
> It was not an important issue.
> It was a trifling issue.
>
> She was not confident of her success.
> She distrusted her success.
>
> Don't use *not* too often.
> Avoid *not* wherever possible.

ERROR #7: *One*

Many teachers of formal writing will tell students to avoid using the first person pronoun *I*. This is silly. Of course, you want to avoid sprinkling "I think" or "it is my opinion" all over the place. The first person is much more noticeable in writing than in speech. Too many *I*'s make you sound like an egomaniac. On the other hand, nothing is more noticeable than substituting the awkward *one*. Americans tend to sound very stuffy when they use it since, unlike the British, they don't use it much in common speech. It is better to say, "I surveyed five hundred college students and discovered ..." than to say, "When one surveys five hundred college students, one finds that ...". To avoid both, draft using the first person. When you polish, cut out every *I* possible. If the *I* is unavoidable, leave it alone.

ERROR #8: Buzz words

Avoid buzz words like *socialize, impact, compact, interface, finalize, interpersonal, personalize, input, output, feedback, implement*—the list is nearly endless. Most buzz words are pieces of jargon borrowed from the sciences or professions. In those professions, the words have specific, carefully defined meanings often attributable to the work of one person. Different professions may use the same jargon to describe different phenomena. *Feedback* means one thing to the acoustics engineer, another to the computer programmer.

Sometimes, jargon is required for one professional to talk with other professionals without wasting words. Avoid it if you can. Even when you do use it for a purpose, give a quick definition. ("Socialization, the process by which children learn from their parents and peers, is one of the most important concepts in sociology.") If the word has different meanings attached by different researchers, be sure to mention the researcher ("Distributive justice, as defined by John Rawls"). Outside the field, stay away from the jargon. Outside of a sociology paper, *to socialize* means to have a party. Why not just say "have a party?" It's much easier to understand. Instead of "give me your feedback," say "give me your opinion."

One reason for avoiding buzz words is that buzz words are often excuses for not saying something specific. "The new road impacted on the school" is a way to avoid saying "The new road raised the noise on the school playground twenty decibels and made three classrooms unusable." Good writers prefer the specific even when it hurts.

ERROR #9: Misplaced participial phrases

A verb form ending in *ing* is called a participle. A phrase beginning with a participle is called a participial phrase. Participial phrases always modify another word or phrase, usually a noun or noun phrase. They pose no problems as long as you always put participial phrases immediately before or immediately after the word the phrase modifies. If Pat is screaming at a mouse, put the participial phrase just before or just after the word Pat.

Screaming at a mouse, Pat leaped on a chair.

Pat, screaming at a mouse, leaped on a chair.

You don't need to stick like glue to this rule; however, when you don't follow the rule, watch for sentences that sound confusing or downright goofy. It's awfully easy to make chairs scream.

Pat leaped on a chair screaming at a mouse.

Screaming at a mouse, the chair was leaped on by Pat.

ERROR #10: Too much repetition

Most spoken languages are redundant because the speaker needs to make certain that the listener understood the message. One field of mathematics, communications theory, actually studies the amount of redundancy required to make spoken messages clear under varying conditions. Writing should be more compact than speech. The reader can easily review previous points and will notice — and dislike — redundancy. Vigorously cut repetitious words, sentences, phrases, paragraphs, sections, chapters, or even repetitious characters.

Of course, there is nothing wrong with a little repetition to remind readers of a previous point or to make a transition, especially in long pieces covering technical subjects. (You may have noticed that we are repeating here a style rule that we mentioned in the activity on polishing for style. Excessive? Well, we don't think this point can be overemphasized.) Use repetition for a purpose, and don't overdo it. Try cutting out all repetitions first; then sparingly add those needed for reminders or transitions. When in doubt, cut it out.

ERROR #11: Usage errors

When you make a usage error, you have used a word mistaking its meaning. People make them all the time in speaking. They are much more noticeable in written work. As Mark Twain said, "The difference between the right word and the almost right word is the difference between lightning and a lightning bug."

The classic example of a usage error is confusing the word *affect* with *effect*. *Affect* means "to imitate or act like." (Zorro affected a Spanish fop.) *Affect* also means "to influence or to have a bearing on" (His decision to buy stocks affected his portfolio.) *Effect* is commonly used as a noun meaning "a result" (cause and effect). As a verb, it means "to bring about or to accomplish" (He effected a change in his portfolio by buying stocks.) Not all usage errors are so subtle.

Twain was right. Usage errors can be embarrassing, so check the dictionary for *any* word whose meaning troubles you. You might check Phyllis Martin's *The Word Watcher's Handbook* as well.

ERROR #12: *Who, which, that*

When you use the words *who, which,* and *that,* watch it! *Who* always refers to people; *which* refers to things, and *that* can refer to either people or things. Change "the girl which saw the accident" to "the girl who saw the accident" or to "the girl that saw the accident." (For more information on when to use *that,* see restrictive clauses in the "Practical Punctuation Filesheet," p. 159.)

What about animals? Well, unless they are fictional characters with names and personalities, treat animals as things (the bunny which ate my radishes). What about corpses? This is getting silly. Presumably, it would depend on whether you want to present the corpse as a person or a thing.

ERROR #13: Ambiguity

A baker's dozen has thirteen loaves, and our dirty dozen has thirteen errors. Ambiguities can crop up even in sentences where the usage is precise and the punctuation perfect. How about, "Our mothers bore us?" Which sense of bore did you mean? how about "Our dog eats anything and especially loves children?" Ambiguities are both the funniest errors and the hardest for the writer to spot. Friends will see them easily. They will kid you about them, but you can join in the fun as long as they tease you before it is too late to repair the damage. Double-check every sentence for ambiguities; then ask your friends to check. Even the perfect sentence should be changed if it confuses or unintentionally amuses an intelligent reader.

THE PARTS OF A SENTENCE (FILESHEET)

You don't absolutely need to know the names for the parts of a sentence, but knowing a few simple terms sure does help when you try to talk to people about sentences. We'll be brief.

SUBJECTS AND PREDICATES

The simple subject of a sentence is usually a noun or a noun phrase that tells what the sentence is about.

> *Horses* love hay.

> *Humpty Dumpty* fell.

The simple predicate is usually a verb or verb phrase that tells what the subject does.

> Horses *love* hay.

> Humpty Dumpty *fell*.

The simple subject together with all its modifiers is called the *complete subject*. The simple predicate together with all its modifiers is called the *complete predicate*.

> The students who most love horses/are those who most love hay.

> Sylvia and Susan/are twin gorillas.

> The children/squabbled and howled.

An implied subject is a ghost subject. The subject isn't written down, but you can guess what it should be. ([You] Don't do that!)

When you are attempting to find the subject of a sentence, keep an eye peeled for implied subjects.

CLAUSES

Clauses are groups of words in a sentence that have both a subject and a predicate. There are two kinds: *independent clauses* and *dependent clauses*. Independent clauses can stand on their own as a sentence; dependent clauses cannot.

Independent Clause	*Dependent Clause*
the rabbit leaped off the lion's tail	after the rabbit leaped off the lion's tail
Mary laughed	as Mary laughed
fourteen pixilated men danced a jig	because fourteen pixilated men danced a jig

To make a *complete sentence*, you must have at least one independent clause, called the *main clause*.

The rabbit leaped off the lion's tail. (one main clause)

Mary laughed, and fourteen men danced a jig. (two main clauses)

As Mary laughed, fourteen men danced a jig. (one dependent clause, one main clause)

When there is one main clause, it's called a *simple sentence*; two main clauses, a *compound sentence*; one main clause and one dependent clause, a *complex sentence.*

Another way to think about the dependent clauses is to notice that they can't stand alone because they function as parts of speech: nouns, adjectives, or adverbs.

What you said made me laugh. (noun clause)

There are plenty of good writers *who don't know much about grammar.* (adjective clause modifying the noun *writers*)

When salmon spawn, they turn red. (adverbial clause modifying the verb *turn)*

My writing is better *than it used to be.* (adverbial clause modifying the adverb *better*)

PHRASES

Phrases are groups of words that go together for some reason or other. It's the grammarian's way of saying "thingamajig." If it's not a clause, it's a phrase. The easiest to spot are prepositional phrases: phrases that begin with prepositions (under the lamp, over the hill). Phrases can also function as parts of speech.

Writers at play are a boring lot. (noun phrase)

Gaining weight was his main objective. (noun phrase)

He *had seen* it many times. (verb phrase)

Grammar comes *easily and quickly* to those who learn the parts of speech. (adverbial phrase modifying the verb *come*)

The sky was *clear and sparkling.* (adjective phrase modifying the noun *sky*)

OBJECTS

Sometimes a preposition (up, of, for, over, on, etc.) needs another word in order to make sense (up the hill, up the stairs). That other word (hill, stairs) is the *object* of the preposition. Some verbs—not all—also require objects at times; for example, the verb *throw*. In the sentence, "Throw the ball" the word *ball* is the *object* of the verb throw. What about "throw up?" Hmm. Well, the thing to remember about grammar is that the language came first, and the folks who named things and made up the rules came second. That's why there are so many exceptions, and why you must use your ears as well as your head when you discuss sentences.

PRACTICAL PUNCTUATION (FILESHEET)

We don't cover the waterfront of punctuation rules here, but we thought a quick review of the punctuation most practical for the average person might help you. (If your eyes tend to close when you read punctuation rules, try writing your own versions of the examples as you read. Practice one rule at a time. You need to stay awake to learn punctuation rules.)

1. A PAIR OR A SERIES OF WORDS, PHRASES, OR DEPENDENT CLAUSES

Conjunctions (and, but, or, not, yet, either ... or, neither ... nor, not ... only, but ... also) join together things that are equal. They join a word to a word; for example, noun to a noun (cats and dogs), verb to a verb (laughs and whines), or adjective to an adjective (funny but sad). Conjunctions can also join a phrase to a phrase (after work but before dinner) or a dependent clause to a dependent clause (since we watched the storm and before the rain stopped). We'll take up joining independent clauses next. For now, let's stick to words, phrases, and dependent clauses.

Here's the rule: You don't need any commas to join a pair of words, phrases, or dependent clauses with a conjunction; however, you must use commas to join series of three or more words, phrases, or dependent clauses with a conjunction.

A pair of nouns: *Dogs and cats* fight.

A series of three: *Dogs, cats, and horses* are domesticated animals.

A pair of verbs: The serious writer *laughs and whines* by turns.

A series of four: The serious writer *laughs, whines, weeps, and wails* once an hour.

A pair of prepositional phrases: I nap *after work and before dinner.*

A series of three: *After work, after a nap, and before dinner* I take time to write down my hopes for tomorrow.

A pair of dependent clauses: The tourist *who chose the right envelope and who won a million dollars* came from Mars.

A series of dependent clauses: The tourist *who chose the right envelope, who won a million dollars, and who flew home the next day* came from Mars.

One exception: If the phrases or clauses are not too complicated, and you also use a conjunction between each word in the series, you can eliminate the commas.

Dogs and cats and horses fight.

If you are unsure if your series is simple or not, it's probably not. Use the commas.

You may be confused by the rule for series because you have seen series written "dogs, cats and horses." When it is a simple series, some people eliminate the comma before the conjunction *and*. Don't follow their lead. Always put in the comma before the *and*. It's too easy to accidentally confuse your reader by writing something like this: "I could never understand the psychology of dogs, cats and horses and never will." This sentence probably needs to be completely revamped, but short of rewriting it, putting a comma after *cats* would help.

2. PAIRS OF INDEPENDENT CLAUSES

The rules for punctuating pairs changes with independent clauses. Although you do not put a comma before the conjunction joining a pair of words, phrases, or dependent clauses, you *do* put a comma before a conjunction joining a pair of independent clauses.

Clause 1: Mary visited Arizona   Clause 2: she liked Tucson

Mary visited Arizona, and she liked Tucson.

Mary visited Arizona, but she disliked Tucson.

Mary not only visited Arizona, but she also liked Tucson.

There is an exception: When the independent clauses are very short and closely related, you can leave out the comma if you wish.

The birds sang *and* the insects chirped.

People get most confused with the rule for joining independent clauses when they have compound subjects and predicates. Just because you have two subjects and two predicates does not necessarily mean that you are joining two independent clauses.

Mary visited Arizona *and* saw Tucson. (*And* joins "visited Arizona" with "saw Tucson," two predicates.)

Mary *and* Jim visited Arizona. (*And* joins *Mary* and *Jim*, two subjects.)

Mary *and* Jim visited Arizona *and* saw Tucson. (In this sentence the first *and* joins two subjects whereas the second *and* joins two predicates.)

Mary visited Arizona, and Jim saw Tucson. (In this sentence, the *and* joins two independent clauses.)

3. WRITING A SERIES OF INDEPENDENT CLAUSES

To write a series of independent clauses, follow the same rules as you would for all other series.

Mary visited Tucson, Jim saw Flagstaff, and Jodie stayed home.

Again, when the clauses are simple and you also use a conjunction between each clause, you may eliminate the commas.

They came *and* they ate *and* they left.

When you join independent clauses, you have another option: the semicolon, to the mysteries of which we now turn.

4. USING THE SEMI-COLON TO JOIN INDEPENDENT CLAUSES

You can tighten up some sentences by using the semi-colon to replace conjunctions.

Replace this: Mary visited Tucson, and Jim saw Flagstaff.

With this: Mary visited Tucson; Jim saw Flagstaff.

You can also use the semi-colon in a series as follows:

Replace this: Mary visited Tucson, Jim saw Flagstaff, and Jodie stayed home.

With this: Mary visited Tucson; Jim saw Flagstaff; Jodie stayed home.

Or with this: Mary visited Tucson; Jim saw Flagstaff, and Jodie stayed home.

One of the things you should do when you use semi-colons is to make the clauses parallel. When are clauses parallel? When the clauses are constructed along similar lines.

Mary visited Tucson and *Jim saw Flagstaff* are parallel clauses.

Mary visited Tucson and *Jim decided that he would visit Flagstaff* are not parallel clauses.

You can write "Mary visited Tucson; Jim saw Flagstaff," but you would be better off to write "Mary visited Tucson, but Jim decided that he would visit Flagstaff."

You may have read or heard that you should avoid using *then, however, thus, hence, indeed, accordingly, besides, for example,* and *therefore* as the first word in a sentence. When, however, you want to use these words as the first word of a sentence, the semi-colon provides you with a nice little loophole.

Use the semi-colon for variety; *however,* don't overdo it.

I never listened to the part about semi-colons; *besides,* I never use them anyway.

You can overcome writing blocks in many ways; *for example,* practice everything in a private journal until you feel comfortable before going public

5. JOINING A DEPENDENT CLAUSE WITH AN INDEPENDENT CLAUSE

Remember that a dependent clause always begins with certain words; for example, *when, if, after, before, because, since, once,* etc. Don't forget that a dependent clause, like all clauses, has a subject and a predicate. *Before he left for class* is a dependent clause, but *before class* is a prepositional phrase.

Dependent clause: when (if, after, before, because, etc.) Jim finished his homework

Independent Clause: his friends cheered

Where you place the commas depends on where you put the dependent clause. If it begins the sentence, place the comma after the dependent clause. If it breaks into the middle of the sentence, place commas on either side of the clause. If it ends the sentence, don't use a comma at all.

When Jim finished his homework, his friends cheered. (beginning)

His friends, *when Jim finished his homework*, cheered. (middle)

His friends cheered *when Jim finished his homework*. (end)

6. PARENTHETICAL EXPRESSIONS

Enclose parenthetical expressions in commas. (Don't let the word *expression* throw you. All it means is "a word, a phrase, or a clause.") Parenthetical expressions are additional words, phrases, or clauses tossed into the middle of a sentence for some reason. In other words, parenthetical expressions are expressions you can cross out and never miss.

The dog, *Spot*, loved pickles.

The teacher, *who was nervous*, took a deep breath and launched into a detailed explanation of linear equations.

The best moments of life are, *of course*, a matter of opinion.

The writer, *thrilled with the scene*, rushed to finish.

Naturally, should the parenthetical expression start the sentence, you will not need the left-hand comma; just the right. On the flip side, when the expression ends the sentence, you won't need the right hand comma; just the left.

Singing bawdy songs in full voice, the crowd stayed late into the evening.

He never saw the man before, *at least not before that night*.

7. RESTRICTIVE EXPRESSIONS

Don't enclose restrictive expressions with commas. Restrictive expressions generally begin with the words *that, who,* and *which*. This can be a little confusing because the word *that* always begins a restrictive expression, but the words *who* and *which* can begin either a restrictive expression or a parenthetical one.

The rule for expressions beginning with *that* is easy: No commas. Ever. If you spot , that in your draft, you know you have it wrong because *that* always begins a restrictive expression.

"What about expressions beginning with *which* and *who*?" you ask. Well, whether or not you enclose the expression in commas depends on what you want to say. Suppose you have the following two sentences:

The teacher, *who was nervous*, launched into an explanation of linear equations.

The teacher *who was nervous* launched into an explanation of linear equations.

These two sentences don't mean quite the same thing. In the first sentence the expression *,who was nervous,* is used parenthetically. The sentence is about a teacher who just happens to be nervous. In the second sentence the expression *who was nervous* is used restrictively. The sentence points to the particular teacher who was nervous, as opposed to another teacher (or a group of teachers) who presumably is not nervous. How does one decide? You're the writer. Sometimes, the difference between a parenthetical expression and a restrictive one is a close call. You must decide what you mean to say and punctuate accordingly.

Because you decide close cases, you should not normally encounter problems with restrictive expressions. If, however, you set up a classroom scene with just one teacher in it, and then write the restrictive "The teacher who was nervous," your reader will start hunting for the other teachers. What happened to the teachers who were not nervous?

Not all restrictive expressions begin with *that, who,* or *which.* If you wish to mention that a dog happens to be named Spot, you can use the parenthetical commas: "The dog, Spot, loved pickles." If, however, you wish to point out one particular dog in a group of dogs, the one named Spot, you can write it restrictively: "The dog Spot loved pickles."

8. USING APOSTROPHES TO MAKE THE POSSESSIVE

The apostrophe gives people fits when it is used to make the possessive. It shouldn't, because there are only two rules, and minor exceptions.

Rule 1: When the word means "belonging to one person or one thing" (the singular possessive), add an apostrophe *s* (*'s*).

one minute's thought	John Harrington's house
John's house	the boy's story
a pig's sty	the writer's craft

This same rule applies even to words ending in *s* or *z*.

Marion Jones's house	the waitress's tip
the mattress's coils	the mountain pass's altitude
Alcatraz's inmates	

Rule 2: When the word means "belonging to more than one person or thing" (the plural possessive) and ends in *s* or *es*, just add an apostrophe.

several minutes' thought	the Harringtons' house
the boys' stories	the pigs' sty
the writers' convention	the Joneses' house
ten waitresses' tips	many mattresses' coils

When the plural does not end in *s* or *es*, add an apostrophe *s* (*'s*).

the men's shower	the women's poetry

There are exceptions, and since they manage to confuse everyone, let's straighten them out. First, the possessive pronouns follow their own rules: *my, our, your, his, hers, its,* and *their.* Just memorize them. Second, certain names for ancient figures, such as *Ulysses, Moses,* or *Jesus* are written *Ulysses' boat,* or *Jesus' teachings.* There is no logical reason for this exception. It is just an historical artifact. Unless the person is an historical figure from Roman times or earlier, follow the traditional rules.

THE PERSONALITY OF PUNCTUATION (FILESHEET)

punctuation is not something that you must use because somebody made up some dumb rules and said that you gotta use them punctuation is part of your writing it helps your reader understand what you are saying when you speak you put in punctuation by pausing or by changing the way you say something but you cant do that when you write the only way to make your reader understand is to put in some punctuation stories without punctuation are very very hard to read as you can see.

Instead of thinking of punctuation as rules, try thinking of each piece of punctuation as a person who helps your reader.

Good old Joe, the period

When do you need Joe, the period? At the end of a sentence. Listen to your sentences as you read aloud. When you reach the end of a sentence (you can *hear* it), put in the period. Start the next sentence with a capital letter. Good old Joe is always around. He is relaxed, and he keeps your reader from feeling frantic, breathless, confused, and all strung together.

Jeeves, the comma

Jeeves, the comma, is an excellent butler — the kind you miss when he isn't there but hardly notice when he is. He performs many duties. He puts a very little pause in the sentence to separate words, phrases, or clauses. In fact, Jeeves is so quiet, yet so busy, that it takes quite awhile to learn when to use the comma. Below are some sample sentences to give you some ideas:

Punch, the puppet, is famous in England.
"Punch the puppet!" chanted the crowd.
That's a pretty small rabbit.
That's a pretty, small rabbit.
Whatever happens, happens because of you.
John, who is interested in jazz, bought concert tickets.
The old house, clearly not used for many years, was the gang's favorite hideout.
Jane and Bob, puffing and groaning, finally reached the top of the hill.
Why, Lindy, did you mail the letter without a stamp?
Why Lindy! What a surprise to see you.
They bought baseball bats, balls, and uniforms.
That quilt is black, white, and green.
Did you bring soda pop, potato chips, or hot dogs?
All we ever do is punctuate, punctuate, punctuate!
The dog howled, and the cat meowed.
The dog howled, the cat meowed, and the mouse squeaked.
After the dog howled, the cat meowed.
If the dog howled, the cat meowed.
Since the dog howled, the cat has meowed, and a mouse squeaked.
Because the dog howled, the cat meowed.
While the dog howled, the cat meowed, and the mouse squeaked.

The loudmouth question mark

The *rule* is to put a question mark at the end of a question. The *truth* is that the question mark has a loud, irritating voice. Before you use the question mark, decide how loud you want the question to be. Use a period for soft, quiet questions.

Sally, the semicolon

Sally is shy, and most people don't get to know her, but Sally is very efficient and helpful—a good friend to writers. Sally can replace ", and" for connecting sentences.

She went to the door, and he went to the window, and the rest of us stayed put.

She went to the door; he went to the window; the rest of us stayed put.

The kibitzers, dashes, and parentheses

When you use a phrase enclosed by dashes or parentheses, picture one of the people in the piece stopping the action, turning to the audience, and explaining something. The dash is briefer, less of a break than the parenthesis. You can use commas to pause instead of dashes. Be careful (sometimes these pauses are about as welcome as a backseat driver) with dashes and parentheses. Use them only when you want a break in the action.

It was a beautiful day, we all thought, for a softball game.

It was a beautiful day—we all thought—for a softball game.

It was a beautiful day (we all thought) for a softball game.

The interrupter, the ...

If a character is speaking and is interrupted, you write ... The "..." is called an ellipsis. It indicates an interruption, a speech trailing off, or missing words.

"Billy Jo, I got that goat out of the garage. It ..."
"What goat?" Billy Jo asked. "Why would somebody keep a goat in the garage?"

Marallee put her foot in the stirrup and vaulted onto the horse. "Not bad for an amateur," she thought. "This is fun. I wonder how long George is going to take to ... Gosh, this horse is big."

Now, the interrupter can be extremely irritating. Use the ellipsis (...) only when you don't mind your reader feeling just a little irritated at the interruption.

!, the BOMB!!!

If the world just blew up, use the exclamation point. Otherwise, avoid it. Beginners always use too many!!!!!

The world blew up!

The world almost blew up.

The world could blow up?

:, the drill sergeant

The colon helps you get to the point fast. When you bring on the colon, your reader stands and salutes.

There are three colors of shoes on that shelf: purple, green, and pink.

Buy all of the school supplies on the list below:

There is a reason I never use colons: I always forget the rules.

If you are going camping, don't forget the essentials: food, warm clothing, and a good book.

Remember drill sergeants wear people out, so don't wear your reader out with too many colons. For example, the punctuation is correct in all the sentences below. But the colon really stops the action. The ! stops it too, but not as much. The dash and the comma stop it even less. Use the colon only when you want abrupt halts.

Hey you: the one with the purple tennis shoes.

Hey you! The one with the purple tennis shoes.

Hey you—the one with the purple tennis shoes.

Hey you, the one with the purple tennis shoes.

Notes from the Pros:
On Spelling and Writing

Curiously, spelling poses a particular problem for writers. The English language with its huge vocabulary and flexibility is one of the most beautiful languages for writing, but its spelling is a mess. In English, the sound of words is not consistently connected with the spelling, nor do any rules consistently apply. Despite numerous attempts at spelling reform and a thousand efforts to teach this hodge-podge "scientifically," the only way to learn to spell an English word is to memorize how it looks, ignoring for the most part how it sounds.

Spelling favors people who remember how words look (visual memory). It penalizes those who remember how they sound (auditory memory). The best spellers are those with good visual memory and poor auditory memory. The next best are those with good visual memory and good auditory memory. Worse of all are those poor souls with a good auditory memory but poor visual memory: they'll be labeled as "bad spellers" all of their lives.

Drafting, by contrast, favors auditory memory. Writing is like singing. Remembering the sound and the flow of words helps writers draft realistic dialogue, write musical description and metaphors, and structure fluent sentences. Unfortunately, those with great natural talent for writing are often poor spellers. Mark Twain is a classic example. He couldn't spell his way off the Mississippi, yet his ear for American English was so acute that he laid the foundation for American literature the day *Huckleberry Finn* was published.

By separating polishing from revision, taking on the spelling as an isolated task, and getting help from someone who does not make the same errors as you, you'll have the best chance of finding all the spelling errors. If you fall into the "bad speller" category, don't worry about it too much. Make friends with good spellers. Take them to dinner. Marry one if possible. Ask them to double-check your spelling without giving you a hard time about it. But don't let poor spelling keep you from writing.

Notes from the Pros:
On Manuscripts

The people who read manuscripts—teachers, editors, and contest judges—share a common fate: reading hundreds of manuscripts on a sunny weekend when they would rather go for a hike, take the kids to the zoo, or curl up with a good mystery. It's true. Most of these people haven't the time to read manuscripts during the work week. They do it in their spare time. If you faced such a chore, what would you do? First job: sort out the trash. Put all the manuscripts scribbled on notebook paper in the "loser" pile. Once the losers have lost, you are free to read the professionally-prepared manuscripts to find the best. An attractive manuscript won't necessarily win you a good grade, first prize, or publication, but it will keep you out of the loser pile. You put a lot of work into your writing; the last place you want it to wind up is in the loser pile. To avoid the loser pile, think of the person who will read your manuscript while you prepare it, and make life as easy as possible for that reader.

If you have never read a hundred manuscripts over a weekend, you cannot imagine what it does to one's eyes. These people are touchy about their eyesight. They make their living reading and appreciate a writer who cares about their vision. Always use the highest quality 20# plain white bond paper you can afford for manuscripts. Don't use erasable bonds; it smears. Don't use flimsy paper; it's hard to handle. Use the blackest, crispest ribbons available. Carbon ribbons are best; brand new nylon ribbons next best. Elderly ribbons with little ink left will earn you a place in the loser pile. If you use a word processor, avoid dot matrix printers. Most publishers and many contests won't accept them. Most teachers will, but not enthusiastically. If you can't avoid using a dot matrix printer, at least use a fresh ribbon.

A few other things will earn you a place in the loser pile, too. Watch out for them. *Single spacing*: Manuscripts are double-spaced, typed on one side of the page. No exceptions. *Not following the rules*: If the contest rules tell you *not* to put your name on the piece, putting your name on it will automatically disqualify you. If your professor asks that you not exceed thirty pages, a forty page manuscript will not make you popular. *Typos*: A few typing errors may be acceptable, but scads of typing errors — especially uncorrected typing errors — may mark you as a loser. If you are a lousy typist, consider using a word processor or hiring a typist. *Missing the deadline*: You can miss deadlines, provided you have discussed the problem with your teacher or your editor and made arrangements long before deadline date, and they are not counting on you. Otherwise, you lose.

You can save yourself a good deal of time preparing the manuscript if you think your presentation through before you tackle the typewriter. How are you going to handle the title? A special title page? What about subtitles? Centered? All caps? Underlined? Will you have more than one kind of subtitle? How will each be different? What about examples and illustrations? Indented? How many spaces? What format will you use for footnotes and the bibliography? The more complex your manuscript, the more planning you need to do to keep everything consistent. Inconsistencies in your format annoy and may confuse readers.

Now consider this: What would happen if the editor or teacher dropped a pile of manuscripts? Would Old Butterfingers be able to fish your piece out of the mess and put it back together? Make sure the pages are numbered and every page has a shortened version of the title on it.

You have invested plenty of time in that manuscript; where's your insurance? Thomas Carlyle had to rewrite his masterpiece *The French Revolution* when the only copy of the manuscript was accidentally burned. If copy machines had been invented in his lifetime, he would have bought the first one. Never give a manuscript to anyone without making a copy. Manuscripts are lost, burned, and stolen. They become victms of spilled coffee and plates of spaghetti. We know one writer whose near-complete manuscript was thrown out the window by a burglar! Your only insurance against such disasters is an extra copy in your files. Make that two copies.

Good luck. You've earned it!

Bibliography

Adelman, Robert H. *What's Really Involved in Writing and Selling Your Book*. Los Angeles: Nash Publishing, 1972.

Asimov, Isaac. *The Book of Facts*. New York: Grosset and Dunlap, 1979.

Baker, Samm Sinclair. *Writing Nonfiction That Sells*. Cincinnati, Ohio: Writer's Digest Books, 1986.

Bartlett, John. *Bartlett's Familiar Quotations*. Secaucus, N.J.: Citadel Press, 1983.

Bates, Jefferson D. *Writing with Precision, How to Write So That You Cannot Possibly Be Misunderstood*. Washington, D.C.: Acropolis Books, 1983.

Block, Laurence. *Writing the Novel from Plot to Print (A Step-by-Step Guide from Idea through Outline to the Final Sale)*. Cincinnati, Ohio: Writer's Digest Books, 1986.

Bocca, Geoffrey. *You Can Write a Novel*. Englewood Cliffs, N.J.: Prentice-Hall, 1983.

Boeschen, John. *Freelance Writing for Profit: A Guide to Writing and Selling Nonfiction Articles*. New York: St. Martin's Press, 1982.

Boggess, Louise. *Article Techniques That Sell*. San Mateo, Calif.: B & B Press, 1978.

Boles, Paul Darcy. *Story-crafting*. Cincinnati, Ohio: Writer's Digest Books, 1984.

Brady, John. *The Craft of Interviewing*. Cincinnati, Ohio: Writer's Digest Books, 1976.

Brande, Dorothea. *Becoming a Writer*. Los Angeles: J. P. Tarcher, 1981.

Bregonier, Reginald, and David Fisher. *What's What: A Visual Glossary of the Physical World*. New York: Ballantine Books, 1982.

Buzan, Tony. *Use Both Sides of Your Brain*. New York: E. P. Dutton, 1983.

Carroll, Lewis. *Alice in Wonderland*. New York: Putnam Publishing Group, 1986.

Charlton, James, ed. *The Writer's Quotation Book: A Literary Companion*. New York: Penguin Books, 1981.

Cheney, Theodore A. Rees. *Getting the Words Right: How to Revise, Edit & Rewrite*. Cincinnati, Ohio: Writer's Digest Books, 1984.

The Chicago Manual of Style: For Authors, Editors, and Copywriters. 13th ed. Chicago: University of Chicago Press, 1982.

Collins, Wilkie. *The Moonstone*. New York: Paperback Library, 1966.

Cook, Claire Kehrwald. *The MLA's Line by Line: How to Edit Your Own Writing*. Boston: Modern Language Association of America and Houghton Mifflin Co., 1985.

Cross, Peter R., ed. *Write a Teacher-Aid Book*. Belmont, Calif.: Fearon-Pitman Publishers, 1978.

Daniels, Harvey A. *Famous Last Words: The American Language Crisis Reconsidered*. Carbondale and Edwardsville, Ill.: Southern Illinois University Press, 1983.

Dean, John F. *Writing Well: 60 Simply-Super Lessons to Motivate and Improve Students' Writing*. Belmont, Calif.: David S. Lake Publishers, 1985.

Delton, Judy. *The Twenty-Nine Most Common Writing Mistakes and How to Avoid Them*. Cincinnati, Ohio: Writer's Digest Books, 1985.

Doyle, Michael, and David Straus. *How to Make Meetings Work: The New Interactive Method*. New York: Berkley Publishing Group, 1976.

Edwards, Betty. *Drawing on the Right Side of the Brain: A Course in Enhancing Creativity and Artistic Confidence*. Los Angeles: J. P. Tarcher, 1979.

Edwards, Charlotte. *Writing from the Inside Out*. Cincinnati, Ohio: Writer's Digest Books, 1984.

Elbow, Peter. *Writing with Power: Techniques for Mastering the Writing Process*. New York: Oxford University Press, 1981.

Evans, Bergen. *Dictionary of Quotations*. New York: Delacorte Press, 1968.

Fader, Daniel. *The New Hooked on Books, How to Learn and How to Teach Reading and Writing with Pleasure*. New York: Berkley Books, 1982.

Francis, Dick. *The Racing Game (Odds Against)*. New York: Pocket Books, 1984.

_____. *Reflex*. New York: Fawcett Crest, 1982.

Goldberg, Hirsh. *The Blunder Book*. New York: Quill/William Morrow, 1984.

Goldberg, Natalie. *Writing Down the Bones: Freeing the Writer Within*. Boston: Shambhala Publications, 1986.

Graves, Donald H. *Writing: Teachers and Children at Work*. Portsmouth, N.H.: Heinemann Educational Books, 1983.

Griffith, Benjamin W. *A Pocket Guide to Literature and Language Terms*. Woodbury, N.Y.: Barron's Educational Series, 1986.

Herriot, James. *All Creatures Great and Small*. New York: St. Martin's Press, 1972.

Hodge, John C. and Mary E. Whiten. *Harbrace College Handbook*. New York: Harcourt Brace Jovanovich, 1986.

Holt, John. *Freedom and Beyond*. New York: Dell Publishing Co., 1973.

_____. *The Underachieving School*. New York: Dell Publishing Co., 1970.

Horowitz, Louise. *Knowing Where to Look: The Ultimate Guide to Research*. Cincinnati, Ohio: Writer's Digest Books, 1984.

Hudson, Kenneth. *The Dictionary of Even More Diseased English*. Chicago: Academy Chicago, 1983.

Kane, Eileen. *Doing Your Own Research: How to Do Basic Descriptive Research in the Social Sciences and Humanities*. London: Marion Boyars, 1985.

Kennedy, X. J., and Dorothy M. Kennedy. *The Bedford Reader*. Bedford, Tex.: Bedford Books, 1984.

Kipling, Rudyard. *Just So Stories*. New York: Macmillan, 1982.

Klauser, Henriette Anne. *Writing on Both Sides of the Brain: Breakthrough Techniques for People Who Write*. San Francisco: Harper & Row, 1986.

Knapp, Daniel, and John Dennis. *Writing for Real*. Englewood Cliffs, N.J.: Prentice-Hall, 1972.

Lamm, Kathryn. *10,000 Ideas for Term Papers, Projects, Reports and Speeches*. New York: Arco, 1984.

Leavitt, Hart Day, and David A. Sohn. *Look, Think & Write, Using Pictures to Stimulate Thinking and Improve Your Writing*. Lincolnwood, Ill.: National Textbook, Co., 1986.

Lewis, Norman. *Word Power Made Easy, The Complete Handbook for Building a Superior Vocabulary*. New York: Pocket Books, 1979.

Macrorie, Ken. *Twenty Teachers*. New York: Oxford University Press, 1984.

Madsen, Sheila, and Bette Gould. *The Teacher's Book of Lists*. Santa Monica, Calif.: Goodyear Publishing Co., 1979.

Martin, Harold C. *The Logic & Rhetoric of Exposition*. New York: Rinehart & Company, 1958.

Martin, Phyllis. *Word Watcher's Handbook: A Deletionary of the Most Abused and Misused Words*. New York: St. Martin's Press, 1982.

Matzen, Robert. *Research Made Easy: A Guide for Students and Writers*. New York: Bantam, 1987.

McGinnis, Alan Loy. *Bringing Out the Best in People: How to Enjoy Helping Others Excel*. Minneapolis, Minn.: Augsburg Publishing House, 1985.

Mencken, H. L. *The American Language*. New York: Alfred A. Knopf, 1986.

Morris, William, and Mary Morris. *Morris Dictionary of Word and Phrase Origins*. New York: Harper & Row, 1977.

Murray, Donald M. *A Writer Teaches Writing*. Boston: Houghton Mifflin, Co., 1985.

The New American Desk Encyclopedia. New York: New American Library, 1984.

Owen, David. *None of the Above: Behind the Myth of Scholastic Aptitude*. Boston: Houghton Mifflin, Co., 1985.

Panati, Charles. *Extraordinary Origins of Everyday Things*. New York: Harper & Row, 1987.

Paulsen, Gary. *Dogsong*. New York: Bradbury Press, 1985.

Peter, Lawrence J. *Peter's Quotations: Ideas for Our Time*. New York: Bantam Books, 1980.

Phillips, Kathleen C. and Barbara Steiner. *Creative Writing: A Handbook for Teaching Young People*. Littleton, Colo.: Libraries Unlimited, 1985.

Polking, Kirk, Joan Bloss, and Colleen Cannon. *Writer's Encyclopedia*. Cincinnati, Ohio: Writer's Digest Books, 1986.

Provost, Gary. *100 Ways to Improve Your Writing*. New York: New American Library, 1985.

Rico, Gabriele Lusser. *Writing the Natural Way: Using Right-Brain Techniques to Release Your Expressive Powers*. Los Angeles: J. P. Tarcher, 1983.

Rockwell, F. A. *How to Write Plots That Sell*. Chicago: Contemporary Books, 1975.

Rodale, J. I. *The Synonym Finder*. Emmaus, Pa.: Rodale Press, 1978.

Ross-Larson, Bruce. *Edit Yourself: A Manual for Everyone Who Works with Words*. New York: W. W. Norton & Co., 1985.

Saling, Ann. *The Foundations of Fiction*. Edmonds, Wash.: Ansal Press, 1984.

Shute, Nevil. *The Far Country*. London: Pan Books, 1967.

Smart, William. *Eight Modern Essayists*. New York: St. Martin's Press, 1965.

Smith, Frank. "Reading Like a Writer." *Language Arts* 60, no. 5 (May 1983): 558-67.

Stahl, James, ed. *Merlyn's Pen*. East Greenwich, R.I.: Merlyn's Pen.

Strunk, William, and E. B. White. *The Elements of Style*. New York: Macmillan, 1979.

Thomas, Lewis. *The Lives of a Cell: Notes of a Biology Watcher*. New York: Bantam Books, 1975.

Trager, James, ed. *The People's Chronology: A Year-by-Year Record of Human Events from Prehistory to the Present*. New York: Holt, Rinehart and Winston, 1979.

Treat, Lawrence, ed. *Mystery Writer's Handbook*. Cincinnati, Ohio: Writer's Digest Books, 1984.

Tripp, Rhoda Thomas, ed. *The International Thesaurus of Quotations*. New York: Harper & Row, 1987.

Waddell, Marie L., Robert M. Esch, and Roberta R. Walker. *The Art of Styling Sentences: 20 Patterns for Success: How to Write Sentences with Greater Clarity, Variety, and Style*. Woodbury, N.Y.: Barron's Educational Series, 1983.

Waldhorn, Arthur, Olga S. Weber, and Arthur Zeiger, eds. *Good Reading.* 22d ed. New York: New American Library, 1986.

Wallace, Irving. *The Book of Lists #2.* New York: William Morrow & Co., 1980.

Weisberg, Robert. *Creativity: Genius and Other Myths.* New York: W. H. Freeman and Co., 1986.

Whissen, Thomas. *A Way with Words: A Guide for Writers.* New York: Oxford University Press, 1982.

Winokur, Jon, ed. *Writers on Writing.* Philadelphia, Pa.: Running Press, 1986.

Wonder, Jacquelyn, and Priscilla Donovan. *Whole-Brain Thinking: Working from Both Sides of the Brain to Achieve Peak Job Performance.* New York: William Morrow & Co., 1984.

The Writer. Boston: Writer, Inc.

Writer's Digest Magazine. Cincinnati, Ohio: Fletcher Art Services.

Wye, Margaret Enright. *The Complete Guide to Punctuation: A Quick-Reference Deskbook.* New York: Prentice-Hall Press, 1986.

The Yankee. Dublin, N.H.: Yankee, Inc.

Zavatsky, Bill, and Ron Padgett, eds. *The Whole Word Catalogue 2: A Unique Collection of Ideas and Materials to Stimulate Creativity in the Classroom.* New York: Teachers & Writers Collaborative (McGraw-Hill Paperbacks), 1977.

Zinsser, William. *On Writing Well: An Informal Guide to Writing Nonfiction.* New York: Harper & Row, 1985.

Index